Intermediate Punishments

INTERMEDIATE PUNISHMENTS:
Intensive Supervision, Home Confinement and Electronic Surveillance

edited by
Belinda R. McCarthy

Issues in Crime and Justice, Volume 2
Sponsored by the
Academy of Criminal Justice Sciences

CRIMINAL JUSTICE PRESS
a division of
Willow Tree Press, Inc.
Monsey, New York
1987

For Bernie,
whose strength, compassion and humor
sustain Matthew, Megan and me.

First Printing 1987
Second Printing 1988
Third Printing 1988

Library of Congress Cataloging-in-Publication Data

Intermediate punishments.

(Issues in crime and justice ; v. 2)   1. Punishment--United States--Case studies.   2. Imprisonment--United States--Case studies.   3. Probation--United States--Case studies.   4. Rehabilitation of criminals--United States--Case studies. I. McCarthy, Belinda Rodgers.   II. Series: Issues in crime and justice (Monsey, N.Y.) ; v. 2)
HV8693.I58 1987   364.6'8   87-5069
ISBN 0-9606960-4-0 (pbk.)

Table of Contents

Contents

ABOUT THE CONTRIBUTORS

Belinda R. McCarthy is Associate Dean, School of Social and Behavioral Sciences, and Associate Professor of Criminal Justice, University of Alabama at Birmingham.

Richard A. Ball is Professor of Sociology, West Virginia University.

Lawrence A. Bennett is Director, Criminal Prevention and Enforcement Division, U.S. National Institute of Justice.

Thomas G. Blomberg is Professor of Criminology, Florida State University.

Lisa C. Burcroff is Research Assistant, School of Criminology, Florida State University.

James M. Byrne is Associate Professor and Director of the Center for Criminal Justice Research, University of Lowell.

Todd Clear is Associate Professor of Criminal Justice, Rutgers University at Newark.

Donald Cochran is Commissioner of Probation, Commonwealth of Massachusetts.

Ronald P. Corbett, Jr. is Director, Training and Development, Office of the Commissioner of Probation, Commonwealth of Massachusetts.

Christine E. Curtis is Assistant Director of the Criminal Justice Research Unit, San Diego Association of Governments.

Contributors

Suzanne Flynn is Probation Officer and Project Coordinator of the Probation Development Project, Justice Services Department, Multnomah County, Oregon.

Edward J. Latessa is Associate Professor of Criminal Justice, University of Cincinnati.

J. Robert Lilly is Professor of Sociology and Criminal Justice, Northern Kentucky University.

Charles A. Lindquist is Associate Professor of Criminal Justice, University of Alabama at Birmingham.

Frank S. Pearson is Associate Research Professor of Sociology, Institute for Criminological Research, Rutgers University at New Brunswick.

Joan Petersilia is Senior Researcher, The Rand Corporation.

Annesley K. Schmidt is Research Analyst, U.S. National Institute of Justice.

Carol Shapiro is Director of the Program Resources Center, School of Criminal Justice, Rutgers University at Newark.

Joseph B. Vaughn is Doctoral Fellow, Criminal Justice Center, Sam Houston State University.

Gorden P. Waldo is Professor of Criminology, Florida State University.

John T. Whitehead is Associate Professor of Criminal Justice, University of Alabama at Birmingham.

Jennifer Wright is Research Assistant, Northern Kentucky University.

FOREWORD

Thirty years ago, the American Law Institute's new Model Penal Code was regarded as the best thinking of the time, and its ideas were to dominate the development of sentencing policy in this country for the next quarter of a century. That is, they were to dominate until the mid-1970s, when a constellation of forces — partly empirical, partly ideological, partly political — coalesced to dislodge them from their leading place in penological policy in the United States.

As support for the assumptions underlying the Model Penal Code eroded, the question arose: what was to replace them? If rehabilitation, a central function of the code, had lost its position of hegemony, what were the goals that sentencing was now to serve? Deterrence and desert had been used in the Model Penal Code to set the outside limits of punishment. They were not employed as exact mathematical expressions, but rather as relative statements about punishments that were either clearly excessive or overly lenient. They established a range in which the goals of rehabilitation were to be achieved. However, as a result of the attack on the Model Penal Code and rehabilitation, desert began to be employed not as a limiting principle, but instead as a precise scale of penalties to be levied for specific offenses and expressed in a system of determinate sentences.

But as desert became more popular, its realities became more elusive. Its irrelevance to the public's desire for protection against crime is probably the chief reason why no contemporary sentencing system has adopted the approach in its entirety, even though the values attached to deserts have often received legislative lip service. As a matter of fact, desert in many jurisdictions has been, in great measure, replaced by incapacitation, either directly or indirectly, as a favored principle. The emphasis is shifting away from "fairness" and toward the removal of the offender from the community for as long as possible, resulting in an explosive growth in prison populations. This growth, in turn, has highlighted the need to maintain the viability of community supervision for handling many offenders and to develop means to classify them so that those incarcerated can be moved as soon as possible from expensive prison systems to the community.

The issue has become: are there ways that the public can be reasonably assured of its protection while offenders are placed in the community and efforts made to assist them in avoiding future crime? Today, concern for rehabilitation in the community has been matched by a concern for control. A principal method to achieve these ends has been the growth of intensive supervision methods, grounded in classification systems that segregate offenders according to their risk and needs, and the use of new types of supervision programs to maintain public safety. A recent development, in this direction, has been the use of home confinement and electronic surveillance aimed at increasing community safety and other sentencing goals without the use of costly institutionalization.

Belinda McCarthy's book deals with these important contemporary correctional issues in the United States. It is a needed publication that addresses systematically the general issue of intensive supervision and home confinement and electronic surveillance. The issues raised by these approaches, of course, are profound. They involve not only matters of effectiveness and efficiency, but very fundamental questions of appropriateness and fairness as well.

The chapters selected for inclusion in this book are well chosen, and each is worth careful study; however, the introduction alone is worth the acquisition of this work. It is one of the best statements that one will find covering the general background of this field, and is valuable to any person interested in literature or policy. It is not often that one finds a young scholar able to understand, probe, and articulate the issues of such a significant area as well as Professor McCarthy does.

Vincent O'Leary
President, University at Albany,
State University of New York
and Professor of Criminal Justice

Introduction

...the current troubles are self-perpetuating. Without alternative sanctions for serious offenders, prison populations will continue to grow and the courts will be forced to consider probation for more and more serious offenders. Probation case loads will increase, petty offenders will be increasingly "ignored" by the system (possibly creating more career criminals), and recidivism rates will rise. In short, probation appears to be heading toward an impasse, if not a total breakdown, if substantially more funds are not made available to create more prison space. Since that is highly unlikely (and also, we believe, undesirable), alternative, "intermediate" punishments must be developed and implemented.

Granting Felons Probation *(Santa Monica, CA: The Rand Corporation, 1985)*

What Are Intermediate Punishments?

Intermediate punishments are those sanctions that exist somewhere between incarceration and probation on the continuum of criminal penalties. The intermediate punishments discussed in this book include intensive community supervision, home confinement, and electronic surveillance. Intensive supervision and home confinement may be used as joint or independent sanctions; electronic surveillance is a method of enforcing curfews or extended periods of home confinement. For example, intensive supervision programs often involve the use of curfews, which electronic surveillance can be used to enforce. Periods of home confinement beyond the limits of curfews may also be a part of intensive supervision programs. Home confinement, with or without electronic surveillance, can be used as an independent sanction, requiring no supervision beyond that necessary to ensure house arrest.

At present, most intensive supervision programs are targeted for felony offenders, while many home confinement programs are designed for misdemeanants. Use of these sanctions reflects the range of dispositions available for felons and misdemeanants; in effect, the continuum into which the penalties must fit. Felons under correctional supervision are typically placed on probation or imprisoned; misdemeanants who merit more severe or different penalties than fines or restitution are typically jailed, since misdemeanant probation is rarely available. The use of intensive supervision stands between regular probation and imprisonment; house arrest is often the only nonfinancial alternative to jail.

1

Many intensive supervision programs are a direct response to prison overcrowding. Prisoners or offenders likely to be incarcerated are targeted for intensive supervision caseloads, usually managed by probation officers. Other intensive supervision programs resulted from the growing use of risk and needs classification schemes with probationers. These tools make possible the planned use of resources by identifying those offenders who need special attention and those who require very little supervision. Home confinement and electronic surveillance of persons under house arrest were originally designed as alternatives to jail. The specific purpose of residential confinement was to punish the offender in a non-financial manner similar to jail both in punitive and incapacitative effect, but at a lower cost.

At this time, the major difference between the strategies is that intensive supervision incorporates aspects of regular probation, such as service delivery, either through resource brokerage or direct provision of assistance from the supervising officer, while home confinement usually does not. Intensive supervision is essentially the offspring of probation, while house arrest is a modified version of confinement. As these strategies receive greater use, we can expect further experimentation with different combinations of strategies and different offender groups. The expansion of home confinement to felony populations, for example, is already under way in many jurisdictions.

Although these intermediate sanctions developed along different lines, they share several important features. First, they are community-based penalties. The offender remains in the community, usually living at the same residence and maintaining existing employment and family ties. Second, they are designed to be humane, but punitive. Because these penalties represent the community's response to at least moderately severe criminal acts, they deliberately impose suffering through the deprivation of liberty. Offenders must adhere to curfews, and accept intense monitoring of their activities at home and elsewhere. Third, these sanctions are expected to protect the community from crime. Through the use of surveillance and curfews, incapacitation is accomplished in a community setting. Fourth, these sanctions are expected to cost less than institutions.

Intermediate Punishments as Community Based Sanctions

During the 1960s and 1970s, community corrections—diversion and pretrial release programs, halfway houses, work and study release, and furloughs, along with the more traditional programs of probation and parole—were widely heralded as panaceas for criminal justice and correctional problems. Community-based programs and facilities were viewed by many observers of the criminal justice system as the best strategies to meet individual offender needs, promote reintegration, and reduce crime. As an added bonus, these programs seemed to cost less than existing practices.

The concern with offender problems and needs has now drastically declined (except perhaps among those correctional workers charged with the supervision of offenders), and the term reintegration seems to have fallen from common usage. Our current conceptualization of the criminal includes some acknowledgment of the inevitability of crime as a part of the human condition, and movement away from the view that crime and other social problems are easily malleable. In the 1980s, the economic advantages of community corrections have shifted from the status of an ancillary selling point to a principal rationale, prompted by an enormous institutional overcrowding problem that repeatedly forces a choice between new construction and the development and utilization of "alternatives."

It should be emphasized, however, that cost-effectiveness is not the only reason for the growing interest in community-based intermediate punishments. The vast majority of "correcting" has always been done in the community, because this is the best place to deal with offenders. While it *can* be the most economical site for dispositions, the community *is* invariably the most humane setting and the richest environment in which to meet offender needs. If community corrections today is suffering from a lack of credibility, it is because we have used many community programs, especially our richest option—probation—unwisely. Too many offenders have been poorly supervised by overworked and undertrained staff, often with a confused sense of purpose. Staff, offenders and the community have suffered as a result.

The search for intermediate punishments is an attempt to find mid-range solutions in the heretofore bipolar correctional continuum. This examination of new strategies and reconsideration of current practices should be taken as a challenge to revitalize probation and other community-based programs. The objective is clear: to ensure that diverse types of offenders supervised in the community are effectively sanctioned and controlled, and that the assistance that community-based programs are most capable of providing is made available to those who can benefit from it.

If community-based programs can be made sufficiently punitive, but in a manner that is neither abusive nor lingering in its effect, then we will have successfully expanded the range of existing penalties to better fit the diversity of criminal behavior. The choice between prison and probation has never been a very satisfactory one, and efforts to shorten prison terms to achieve more mid-range punishments have largely failed. Our only option is to make community sanctions part of our retributive response to crime.

Intermediate Punishments for Purposes of Retribution and Incapacitation

The dominant themes in criminal justice in the 1980s are punishment and community protection. These objectives attained their present levels of significance for a variety of reasons. There has been a loss of faith in rehabilitation, and there is considerable belief that faith alone was at the center of the rehabilitative ideal. There is much evidence that the objectives of treatment have been rarely attained because of severe problems in theoretical conceptualization and program implementation. The acceptance of the ideology of rehabilitation led to an individualization of correctional response that frequently yielded only disparate punishment. The discretion required by the diagnostician was granted to well-intentioned, but ill-prepared correctional workers. With little guidance provided or accountability demanded, the difficult task of treatment became virtually impossible, resulting in hidden costs to offenders and little benefit to the community. Although there is much support today for the provision of services to offenders on a voluntary basis, there is little enthusiasm for the objective of rehabilitation as a dominating purpose in our correctional system.

Although many death penalty enthusiasts believe wholeheartedly in deterrence, the objective of deterrence (like rehabilitation) is generally unacceptable as a basis for sanctioning policy. Few offenders are caught and fewer still convicted, so questions regarding the amount of punishment required to achieve deterrence—the questions that must be addressed in any attempt to develop dispositional policy—are simply unanswerable. Whatever sentences are imposed on serious criminal offenders seem to have little consistent and predictable impact on the behavior of those sentenced or potential offenders. People enter and refrain from crime for reasons largely beyond the control of the sanctioning process.

Punishment and incapacitation have their own strengths and weaknesses as dispositional rationales. Punishment assumes rational actors who have freedom of action and freedom of choice, an attractive conceptualization of man. The proponents of the justice model of corrections have provided additional support for punishment, eloquently arguing for equal punishments for equal crimes. This is an achievable goal. We can punish equitably and we can increase punishments for more severe crimes. If it is fair to fit the punishment to the crime rather than the criminal, then punishment can be fairly administered. By adopting punishment as our objective, we elevate it from its earlier status as the unintended consequence of rehabilitation. We also comfortably shift our attention to proportionality, a seemingly more manageable issue than the broader and more ambiguous questions surrounding sanctioning purpose.

Incapacitation (the physical restraint of criminals for the purpose of preventing crime) rests on somewhat shakier ground and thus tends to be subordinated to punishment in our hierarchy of objectives. Our concern with the protection of the community is clearly appropriate. Our knowledge that a small number of offenders commit much of the crime, and that recidivism rates, especially in urban areas, are extremely high, certainly warrants reasoned protective action when we do have an offender in hand. Undermining these arguments for incapacitation is the unavoidable problem of targeting the dangerous minority for confinement in a manner that saves the non-recidivist from unnecessary incarceration. Although there is now support for "selective incapacitation" (the targeting of chronic high risk offenders for imprisonment), at times it seems to represent merely a new willingness to overlook the problems of prediction.

It might also be argued that our current support for punishment and incapacitation is inextricably tied to present economic and political realities. When state and federal coffers appeared to be full, our policies dictated a search for ways to improve the human condition. Even as crime was increasing, there was great interest in helping communities and individuals solve the problems considered to be at the root of crime. Today, political conservatism dictates budget cutting in social service programs, and there is a greater willingness to punish offenders as rational actors and to lock up those who might threaten the public welfare.

And herein lies the paradox. Given our present willingness to punish, building even more prisons and jails would be the obvious strategies to pursue when the objectives are retribution and incapacitation. But the lack of funds serves as a stimulus for moderation. Just as punishment continued and perhaps expanded through net-widening (the unintended increase in the number of persons sanctioned) during the era of rehabilitation and community corrections, so strategies of moderation continue to develop in an environment willing to accept harsher action.

Intermediate punishments are especially significant in this regard. Whatever the political realities and economic necessities, this society has never had a sufficiently broad range of sanctions to meet the diversity of criminal behavior. We now have an opportunity to establish and test strategies that can have a lasting impact on our ability to fit the punishment to the crime, but we must be certain to deliberately target our populations and keep our central purposes clear.

Intermediate punishments must be used with middle range offenders, and the meaning of "middle range" needs to be examined very carefully. As some of the articles that follow aptly point out, a serious offender in one state may be viewed as only a minor offender in another.

The issues of net-widening and the expansion of social control must also be addressed. The unconscious and unplanned net-widening that occurred under the guise of diversion in the 1960s and 1970s is clearly undesirable and avoidable. However, some net-widening may be appropriate in some jurisdictions. We cannot asume that all jurisdictions are appropriately responding to all types of offenders. For example, if there are offenders who merit punishment but need no supervision, who are currently ignored by our correctional system because neither fines nor jail time is appropriate (such as those who chronically fail to pay child support), house arrest may be a desirable added punishment. Although each jurisdiction must learn from the examples of other communities, each jurisdiction that increases its correctional repertoire will have to conduct careful self-examination.

Intermediate Punishments as Cost Effective Correctional Measures

Intermediate punishments will only save money if they cost less than the alternatives that would have been used in their absence. As the Florida correctional system has demonstrated, prisons can be constructed more economically than in the past. If expense is the major issue, realistic costs of confinement must be used for purposes of comparison. Because minimum supervision costs less than maximum supervision, intensive supervision programs will bring added costs if their caseloads are drawn from the ranks of regular probationers. House arrest will cost more than doing nothing, even if the electronic surveillance technology employed is inexpensive. And if the failures from intermediate punishments receive costly dispositions, then those too must be counted in the costs of the strategy.

All of these factors must be considered when we "cost out" intermediate punishments. Even if intensive supervision programs are developed for the express purpose of removing offenders from incarceration, a review of all supervision levels should be undertaken at the time of program development to ensure that the offenders in the intensive supervision program are indeed the most appropriate for close monitoring, and that other offenders receive no more supervision than they require.

The development, testing and refining of new correctional strategies is no simple task. The correct positioning of these strategies may be even more difficult. Only through careful study and planning can we achieve the re-balancing of cost and social control objectives that the introduction of intermediate punishments requires.

OVERVIEW OF CONTENTS

The articles by Petersilia, Clear, Flynn and Shapiro examine the issues that must be addressed when model intensive supervision programs are evaluated by other jurisdictions. Petersilia focuses on the highly successful Georgia experience, and describes what made the program not only workable, but effective in the context of Georgia corrections. As she points out, although Georgia's target population constitutes mid-range offenders in the Georgia correctional system, these same offenders might be considered "lightweights" in another setting. The reductions in recidivism that Georgia was able to achieve might well be unrealistic for jurisdictions whose mid-range offenders are more serious and chronic offenders. She also describes how Georgia made all the right moves in program development and implementation—the crisis in prison overcrowding was used as a stimulus for reform, the support of key actors ranging from the governor to operational staff was actively recruited, the program was built *for Georgia* after a careful assessment of local conditions, and a sound funding base was established.

Clear, Flynn and Shapiro describe intensive supervision programs in three jurisdictions, and provide a critical examination of the serious issues of offender control and net-widening. Although offender monitoring is a principal focus of intensive supervision, little attention has been given to problems affecting the limits, the range and the failure of control. Only a finite amount of time can be devoted to surveillance; much of an offender's time is going to be uncontrolled no matter how intensive the supervision is. What strategies are needed to support the supervision effort? And how much control should an offender receive given that time spent by the supervising officer in surveillance activities is time lost from the provision of support services? And because monitoring is likely to pick up technical violations that would normally go unobserved, what should be done with the technical violators of intensive supervision? If these violations are ignored, then the credibility of surveillance is damaged. If the violators are harshly punished and institutionalized, then we have added to the correctional dilemma, because their institutionalization may result from the surveillance rather than from intractable criminality. Expanding the reach and degree of punishment to these offenders is a particularly pernicious form of net-widening.

Corbett, Cochran and Byrne provide us with a case study of the change process, describing issues and efforts involved in establishing the Massachusetts Intensive Supervision program. They describe how academics and practitioners worked together in an effort to change the probation system from a rehabilitation-oriented, decentralized and personality driven system to a centralized and standards-governed agency that pursued the objectives of risk control and community corrections. By discussing the theoretical components of change, and describing related steps in the Massachusetts effort, the authors provide stimulating insight into the process of program development and implementation.

Whitehead and Lindquist contribute a new dimension to our understanding of intensive supervision—the perspective of the supervising officer. Their examination of the Alabama intensive supervision program, which employs former prison guards as supervising officers, yields a portrait of supervisors who enjoy their work and are satisfied with their jobs, but are also often unable to provide the assistance offenders really need and tend to take shortcuts in surveillance activities to save time. These officers have tremendous discretionary power, including the power to recommend transfers back to prison and to accept or reject an offender back on their caseload after his return to prison. The social control issues here are formidable.

Frank Pearson addresses the thorny issues of cost and benefit as he describes New Jersey's intensive supervision program and its plans for budget analysis. The proper role of expenditure and revenue statements, and the need to consider opportunity costs are discussed, as are the difficulties of measurement, the importance of multiple analytical perspectives and the need to consider optional levels of program implementation. His comprehensive assessment also examines the potential impact of qualitative benefits such as increased equity in the correctional process and humanitarian concerns.

The concluding articles in this first section are evaluations of intensive supervision programs in Ohio and Wisconsin. Although intermediate punishments are expected to both punish and control, the control objectives and measures of recidivism are invariably the focus of attention when evaluations are conducted. Although neither of these particular evaluations yielded very positive results in reducing recidivism, both studies provide valuable insight into the reasons for limited program effectiveness and the difficulties of conducting empirical research. The article by Latessa describes the problems of developing adequate comparison groups and interpreting the results when there are considerable differences between offenders supervised under experimental and control conditions. The failure to achieve sufficiently intensive levels of supervision and service delivery is detailed and offered as a possible explanation for limited program effectiveness.

The chapter by Bennett describes an extremely well executed research project, which nevertheless failed to significantly reduce offender recidivism. Again, the question is raised "how intense must supervision be to affect the behavior of high risk offenders?" The program did accomplish some of its objectives—supervision was effectively reorganized to better fit risk and need levels, and low risk offenders were successfully supervised with a minimum of resources. These benefits cannot be ignored, but it is clear that experiments in intensive supervision must continue, incorporating varying levels and types of surveillance, and of support service delivery.

The articles on electronic surveillance have much in common with the chapters on intensive supervision. Although there is clearly an added concern over the electronic monitoring technology and its special implications, the issues addressed are basically the same. Under what conditions can the programs accomplish their stated objectives? Are we targeting the right offenders for the programs? What do we do with violators? Can we save money over existing options? And most importantly, are we better off with this program than without it? Although there is always a tendency to answer that last question with a quick "yes" because of our lack of satisfaction with the present, these articles make clear the need to carefully consider the impact of all our options.

Schmidt and Curtis describe the four basic technologies employed in electronic monitoring of offenders and some of the problems that have been encountered in program operation. They evaluate the advantages and disadvantages of the programs, and effectively address the complex question "why monitor?" This is obviously a question that each jurisdiction will need to consider in light of its budget, target offender population and political context.

The State of Texas is carefully planning the introduction of electronic monitoring and home confinement into its range of correctional options. As part of this effort, a study was commissioned on existing programs and technology. Vaughn describes the results of this ten-program study, including a detailed assessment of technological problems (i.e., false alarms, tamper-proofing, who can wear the devices and where they can be used) and cost benefit assessments. The evaluation of these findings led to the conclusion that electronic monitoring should not be employed as a quick fix for a complex problem.

Blomberg, Waldo and Burcroff describe the State of Florida's extensive use of home confinement without electronic surveillance. Home confinement is employed as a sanction for new offenders and as a disposition for misdemeanant and technical violators of probation and parole. The program includes the use of restitution and community service, and restricts offenders to their homes except for employment and activities approved by a home confinement officer. Thus far, it appears that older and more mature offenders adjust more successfully to home confinement.

The Palm Beach County paper differs from the others in that it is not an academic evaluation of programs and issues, but a practitioner's straightforward and unabashedly enthusiastic description of his jurisdiction's experience with electronic surveillance. The Palm Beach County program developed independently of Florida's home confinement effort, and represents one of the first U.S. uses of electronic surveillance as a disposition for misdemeanants. This uncritical description of events and the program's success is especially valuable because it so effectively captures the excitement over electronic surveillance as an alternative to the local jail, an area in which alternatives have been sorely lacking.

The Kenton County, Kentucky electronic surveillance program developed at about the same time as the Palm Beach effort. Lilly, Ball and Wright describe the implementation of the Kentucky program, and address several serious questions about program impact and effectiveness. How many offenders must be placed on home confinement for it to be truly cost effective? How can inappropriate net-widening be avoided? How much time should offenders be required to serve under conditions of home confinement? The difficulty of answering these questions through single site evaluation is clear. Multi-site evaluations are needed if we are to separate what works in one jurisdiction from what can work as a model for all jurisdictions.

CONCLUSION

Intermediate punishments are gaining in popularity faster than we can study them. This tendency for social programs to develop and proliferate before research can address even the most basic programmatic issues is neither new nor specific to corrections. It is part of the inevitable rush of enthusiasm that is generated when any "new" strategy gains some prominence as a solution to questions of social policy. Too often, the less than perfect research outcomes eventually reported not only dampen this enthusiasm, but cripple program growth. There is no need for this to occur with intermediate punishments. If current programs can be viewed as experiments rather than all or nothing tests of program effectiveness, then research can be used to further, rather than impede, program development. The objectives of this research are clear: to establish how these programs are being used and how they can best be used; to determine whether these programs are effective punishments, community control strategies or possibly even therapeutic tools; to identify the mix of retribution and community protection strategies that can best meet our correctional needs; and to identify the issues which make or break programs in different community and correctional contexts.

Intensive supervision, electronic monitoring and home confinement are not panaceas, and they should not be idealized as such, making them vulnerable to any reports of negative or conflicting outcome. These programs represent significant attempts to fill a sanctioning void that has too long been ignored. The program efforts reported here must be followed by further experimentation with dispositions that acknowledge the severity of the criminal act, the rightful concern of the community for the safety of its citizens, the humanity of the victim and the offender, and the limitation of general revenues. In the future, intermediate punishments may be different from the programs we now see developing, but their place in correctional policy should be secure. Having learned that alternatives are possible, traditional "probation or prison" decision-making begins to appear not only simplistic, but unnecessary and unwise.

FOR FURTHER READING

Doleschal, Eugene (1982). "The Dangers of Criminal Justice Reform." *Criminal Justice Abstracts* (March): 133-152.

McAnany, Patrick D., Doug Thomson and David Fogel (1984). *Probation and Justice: Reconsideration of Mission.* Cambridge, MA: Oelgeschlager, Gunn and Hain.

McCarthy, Belinda and Bernard McCarthy (1984). *Community-Based Corrections.* Monterey, California: Brooks/Cole.

O'Leary, Vincent and Todd R. Clear (1984). *Directions for Community Corrections in the 1990's.* Washington, DC: U.S. National Institute of Corrections.

Petersilia, Joan and Susan Turner, with Joyce Peterson (1986). *Prison versus Probation in California.* Santa Monica, CA: Rand Corporation.

Petersilia, Joan, Susan Turner, James Kahan, and Joyce Peterson (1985). *Granting Felons Probation: Public Risks and Alternatives.* Santa Monica, CA: Rand Corporation.

Belinda R. McCarthy

Epilogue to the Second Printing

New research findings on the uses of intermediate punishments produce fresh insight into program operations. The interplay of technology, and the interpersonal dimensions of intermediate punishments, are among the most interesting issues raised by recent research. As we learn about the assets, liabilities and operational difficulties of different types of electronic surveillance systems, the importance of human decision makers in these technologically innovative programs becomes more apparent. A recent evaluation of an electronic surveillance program noted that offender compliance was high even when the hardware was performing poorly, and concluded that "the equipment may contribute to success only to the extent that the probation officer uses it skillfully and thoughtfully."[1]

At this date, there are few reports of resistance to intermediate punishments. The general public seems to welcome the introduction of sentencing options. Families of adult offenders receiving intermediate punishments seem to adjust to the conditions of what can be "mutual confinement" with little difficulty. There are reports that some of these offenders may even experience rehabilitative gains in cases where home confinement necessitates a significant break with the lifestyle that may have contributed to criminal behavior.

Programs serving juveniles are developing rapidly. These efforts can be expected to encounter new and different demands when the problems of adolescence exacerbate the home confinement/intensive supervision situation.

Although the initial writers on electronic surveillance noted a variety of potential problems, little is being said today about the danger inherent in this new form of social control. But the availability of a surveillance technology that is more decentralized, cost-effective, expansive and intrusive than any other form of correctional surveillance ever employed poses clear risks of overuse and misuse, risks that may actually increase as the technology improves. To avoid the pitfalls of "too much of a good thing," each use of the technology should be justified, noting how the hardware contributes to the disposition and permits a more effective and appropriate response to crime than available alternatives. At a minimum, the development and expansion of sentencing alternatives requires a very explicit and deliberate approach to their employment.

1. Annette Jolin, *Electronic Surveillance Program Evaluation, Clackama County Community Corrections* (Oregon City, Oregon, undated).

Part I

Intensive Supervision

Georgia's Intensive Probation: Will the Model Work Elsewhere?

by
Joan Petersilia

Georgia developed an intensive probation supervision (IPS) program in 1982 to respond to prison crowding. The program is widely deemed a success: few participants recidivate, and most are able to pay a probation supervision fee. Other states are rapidly moving to implement programs modeled after Georgia's, hoping for similar results. This article addresses the question: "Will the Georgia program work elsewhere?" The author argues that the transferability of Georgia's IPS is far from assured. Two aspects of Georgia's context seem unique, and related to the IPS program's success: (1) a high prison commitment rate, which has created an eligible pool of prison-bound offenders convicted of less serious crimes, and (2) an extremely supportive and professional local context. Without these conditions present, other locales may not experience the success with IPS that has been present in Georgia.

INTRODUCTION

In most states of the U.S., correctional institutions are so crowded that their living conditions violate eighth amendment guarantees against cruel and unusual punishment. This crowding results primarily, and predictably, from a nationwide increase in serious crime. However, that effect has been aggravated by public demands to "put criminals away," demands that have prompted mandatory and/or determinate prison sentencing statutes in many states. Paradoxically, while the public clamors for more severe sanctions, the concern often fades in the voting booth when tax-payers consider the price of approving measures to construct new, or renovate existing, jails and prisons. Since all but eight states are now under federal court orders to thin the crowding in their existing prisons, more, and more serious, felons may be getting probation sentences.

Unfortunately, most felons don't behave very well under the conditions of traditional probation. This is especially the case in jurisdictions where fiscal cuts and increasing probation caseloads severely limit personal contacts between probation officers and their charges. For example, a 1985 Rand Corporation study of felony probationers in two California counties found that even among those felons who had the least serious crime/criminal record "indexes," over 40 percent were convicted of new crimes. Among the most serious felony probationers, the rate was 66 percent (Petersilia, Turner and Kahan, 1985).

Given prison crowding, the felony probationers' recidivism rates, and the prohibitive cost of building new jails and prisons, I believe, and have frequently advocated, that the country needs some alternative to imprisonment for a certain group of felony offenders. As the Rand study's report states:

> ...the criminal justice system needs an alternative, intermediate form of punishment for those offenders who are too antisocial for the relative freedom that probation now offers, but not so seriously criminal as to require imprisonment. A sanction is needed that would impose intensive surveillance, coupled with substantial community service and restitution. It should be structured to satisfy public demands that the punishment fit the crime, to show criminals that crime really does not pay, and to control potential recidivists. [Petersilia, Turner and Kahan, 1985: ix.]

One alternative is Intensive Probation Supervision (IPS). IPS programs allow offenders to remain in the community under strict surveillance, and usually require them to pay victim restitution, hold a job, submit to random urine and alcohol testing, and pay part of the cost of their supervision. These programs seem to satisfy two goals that have long appeared mutually exclusive: reducing prison populations (and budgets), while punishing offenders in a manner that does not trivialize their crimes. As Massachusetts Chief Justice Edward Hennessey put it: "It costs about $25,000 a year to keep a prisoner locked up. A lot of probation supervision can be bought for that sum" (Hennessey, 1985: 11).

Interest has been spurred by the State of Georgia's experience with an IPS program. Begun in 1982, Georgia's IPS is widely regarded as a success. Data from the program show that its participants have extremely low recidivism rates, and most offenders have been able to maintain employment, make victim restitution, and pay a monthly supervision fee. Probationer fees have made the program totally self-supporting, and it continues to enjoy (and, in fact, foster) positive community-agency links, including new respect for the probation department. The program has repeatedly been expanded and has resulted in spin-off, community-based probation programs (e.g., probation detention centers).

These results have generated a great deal of media and professional interest. The upshot is that many states are rapidly moving to implement programs modeled after Georgia's. In commenting on solutions to prison crowding, the *New York Times* concluded:

> The state that has led the way is Georgia, and the most common new program spreading across the South and the nation is modeled on the Georgia program of intensive probation supervision:...[*New York Times*, December 18, 1985].

A *Washington Post* article called Georgia's IPS "the future of American corrections" (August 16, 1985).

The Rand Corporation recently conducted a mail survey of "Innovations in Probation," which was completed by 120 chief probation officers. This survey showed that IPS is the program most often being implemented across the nation: 40 states now are implementing such programs—and half of these states report modeling their efforts after the Georgia IPS program. (Complete results of this survey, sponsored by the Edna McConnell Clark Foundation, will be published in Spring, 1987.) Although I have frequently used the Georgia program to illustrate the feasibility of IPS, I think the time has come to reconsider, if not apply the brakes to, this wholesale rush to adopt that program. Otherwise, a promising corrections alternative may be killed by unrealistic expectations—and worse, if attempts to replicate the Georgia experience fail, public safety could be jeopardized.

A jurisdiction considering the Georgia model must ask itself two critical questions:

(1) Does it have the same kind of offender "pool" that Georgia has for its IPS program?

(2) Can it create similar conditions for developing and implementing that program?

It may be that the Georgia recidivism rates reflect the deterrent effect of highly punitive sentencing practices in that state and/or an offender population in the IPS program that is less seriously criminal than the offender. "pool" in many other states. Even with a similar pool, programs may not prove as successful unless they approach development and implementation as Georgia's Department of Correction did. Georgia's efforts involved virtual "textbook" strategies for effective adoption of innovative programs. The purpose of this essay is to describe the Georgia experience (utilizing data drawn from Erwin, 1984 and 1986 a, b), and to identify the client and contextual features that have helped make Georgia's IPS program both successful and hard to replicate.

PURPOSE AND STRUCTURE OF GEORGIA'S IPS PROGRAM

As the Georgia Commissioner of Corrections stated: "The IPS program's main intent was to demonstrate that serious offenders could be supervised effectively in the community" (Georgia Dept. of Offender Rehabilitation, 1984). The program's developers recognized that it would never get off the ground unless this was first demonstrated to other agencies of the criminal justice system—especially the courts. Consequently, "the program was designed to convince traditionally tough-minded Georgia judges that some of the offenders they normally sent to prison could be safely managed in the community." The result was called the "toughest form of probation in the United States" (Gettinger, 1983).

In Georgia's IPS program, probation caseloads are restricted to 25 offenders, managed by a supervision team. The team is composed of a surveillance officer, whose main role is to monitor the offender closely, and a probation officer, who provides counseling and has legal authority over the case.

Offenders usually spend 6-12 months under IPS, followed by a year on basic probation. During time under IPS, each offender is ordinarily seen five times per week, sometimes in the department office, usually by the probation officer. This schedule reflects the assumption that intensive contact between staff and probationer will increase deterrence and rehabilitation and reduce rearrests.

Offenders are required to perform 132 hours of community service and be employed in an educational/vocational program full time. Employment is necessary because, like other probationers in Georgia, IPS participants may be required to pay a probation supervision fee of $10 to $50 per month, in addition to fines and restitution previously ordered by the court. Beside these conditions, the probation officer or the judge can (and usually does) impose restrictions such as curfews and frequent, but unannounced, drug or alcohol testing.

In developing the program, administrators decided not to define the target group categorically by crime type but as "serious but nonviolent offenders who, without the intensive supervision option, would have gone to prison in the jurisdiction under which they were sentenced" (Erwin, 1986b: 2). Offenders who are "sentenced to prison or recommended for a prison term in their presentence investigation report" are prime candidates for the program, although courts can sentence offenders directly to IPS. By the end of 1985, 2,322 offenders had been sentenced to IPS, about half of which were "prison amended" cases, and half were "direct IPS sentences." Sixty-eight percent were white; 89 percent were male; about half were under 25 years of age; 43 percent had been convicted of property offenses, 41 percent of drug and alcohol related offenses, and 9 percent of violent personal crimes.

HOW SUCCESSFUL HAS THE PROGRAM BEEN?

In evaluating IPS, the key issue is: "Can offenders who would have been incarcerated be managed on probation without unacceptable risks to the community?" From Georgia's experience, the answer seems to be "yes." According to their self-evaluation:

> The citizens of Georgia have had little reason to fear for their safety at the hands of the 2,322 offenders who have been diverted from prison to IPS supervision...the statistics show that [less than 1 percent] of the IPS probationers have been convicted of any crimes which are categorized as violent personal, although 16% of all the offenders served have been revoked for technical or criminal violations." [Erwin, 1986a: 21.]

Offenders originally convicted of drug-related offenses had the highest success rates (90 percent), followed by property offenders (75 percent); and personal offenders (65 percent).

About half of the violations were for new crimes as opposed to technical conditions, and the majority of new crimes were property offenses. To date, armed robbery is the most serious offense of which an IPS participant has been convicted; only one offender has been convicted of this crime, and no one was injured in that instance. Given these figures, Georgia's IPS is commonly credited with an 80 to 90 percent success rate.

To assess the relative effectiveness of IPS, Georgia analysts identified groups of regular probationers and prisoners who resembled the IPS participants in criminal seriousness. The evaluation then compared the recidivism rates for the three groups and found that: "IPS probationers had a lower rate of reconviction for serious crimes against persons than either the regular probation or incarcerated comparison cohorts'' (Erwin, 1986). The data also show that:

> While many IPS probationers were convicted for possession of marijuana and alcohol-related habitual violator offenses, the most serious new offenses were four burglaries, and one armed robbery in which no one was injured. However, for the ex-prisoner sample, there were 13 burglaries, three aggravated assaults, two rapes and two armed robberies. They presented a strikingly greater risk to the community after release. Even the regular probation sample appeared to present a greater risk to the community than the IPS sample. They committed 8 burglaries, one rape, and two aggravated assaults. This comparison suggests that IPS surveillance provided early detection of uncooperative behavior and/or substance abuse, and effectively removed the danger before citizens were harmed. [Erwin, 1986b: 23.]

One might expect the ex-prisoners to have higher rates of personal crimes. Their prison sentences reflect their higher risk; and, some would argue, the prison experience itself might make them more violent. However, one would not expect the probationers to have higher rates, since they are presumably less serious in the first place. If the basic risk of recidivism for both probationer groups is roughly similar, it would seem that the conditions of IPS do contribute to the higher success rates for its participants.

What makes these rates especially encouraging is the fact that all three groups were tracked for 18 months and that the IPS group was on *basic probation* for 6 to 12 months of that period. Evidently, they did not ''make up for lost time'' once intensive surveillance ended, or their rates might have equalled the other probationers'. This suggests that Georgia is buying a lot of crime prevention with IPS—and that some of it may result from actual rehabilitation of the participants. But what is the state paying for this prevention, relative to probation and imprisonment?

Cost calculations computed by Georgia showed that the average cost for basic probation was $300 per offender, per year. The annual expense for each IPS client is $1,600, which is considerably less than the $9,000 cost per year, per prison inmate. Georgia believes it has saved a minimum of $7,000 per offender diverted through the IPS program.

And that is just the operational cost. If capital costs for construction are included, Georgia estimates the savings per year for each prisoner diverted to IPS is close to $11,000. When preliminary data were presented summarizing the first 18 months of IPS performance, diverting 542 offenders, Commissioner of Corrections David Evans said, ''That is one twenty million dollar prison we did not build.'' According to Erwin (1986a: 24), ''Now, 2332 persons have participated in IPS, the threshold would have been crossed requiring the construction of at least two new prisons at ever-increasing costs."

In sum, the Georgia evaluation concludes, "Intensive supervision was an effective alternative to prison because it allowed offenders who might have been incarcerated to be supervised in the community at a cost effective level, and with little risk to the public. It appears that enough people can be diverted to achieve significant cost savings with no terrible consequences to the community" (Erwin, 1986b: iii).

SOME CAUTIONS FOR REPLICATING
THE GEORGIA EXPERIENCE

There can be little doubt that Georgia's program is working *for Georgia*. The critical question is whether Georgia's IPS program holds promise for other jurisdictions. Is it transferable? Other jurisdictions apparently hope that by adopting an IPS model like Georgia's, they will realize the same benefits: recidivism rates will be lower; most revocations will be for minor rule infractions, with almost no new violent crime; supervision fees will foot most of the bill; probationers will maintain jobs and pay victim restitution, and recidivism rates will remain low even after IPS ends.

These expectations may not be realistic, especially if jurisdictions fail to account for differences in their offender pool and to note the quintessential role that certain elements and strategies have played in making the Georgia experience successful.

The Nature of Georgia's Clients

Other jurisdictions may be setting themselves up for a potentially dangerous fall if they project results simply by looking at the reduced recidivism rates in Georgia. For example, a new bill just introduced in the California Assembly (AB2671) states that:

> Preliminary results of intensive surveillance programs currently piloted in other states have demonstrated a reduced recidivism rate for high-risk offenders from 50 percent to 10 percent. If, for example, a similar reduction in recidivism could be achieved in Los Angeles County alone, the number of felony probation violations could be reduced by 3,300 persons annually. That reduction would significantly ease the pressure on overcrowded prisons, and could save the state approximately 45 million dollars annually.

Discussions with the authors of the bill reveal that they are basing their projections, in large part, on the Georgia IPS experience. They assume that a Georgia-type program could realize a similar reduction in Los

Angeles County. Unfortunately, they have failed to take into account two facts. First, Georgia offenders may not have recidivism rates as high as 50 percent, even for released prisoners. Second, recidivism rates for high risk offenders in Los Angeles County are actually somewhere between 50 and 75 percent, depending on the definitions of "recidivism" and "violations" (Petersilia, Turner and Kahan, 1985).

It is unrealistic to expect an IPS program like Georgia's to bring the Los Angeles rates down as low, unless it is dealing with offenders who have similar "expected" risks of recidivism. And a number of things suggest that the Georgia IPS program may be dealing with offenders whose risk is unusually low, by national standards.

Georgia does not have determinate or presumptive sentencing guidelines in effect. Its judges are permitted a great deal of sentencing discretion and, like most other southern judges, they are considered harsh. By the end of 1984, Georgia had a higher percent of its adult population under some form of correctional supervision than any other state in the nation. The average rate nationally is 1.5 percent; for Georgia, it is 3.2 percent (Bureau of Justice Statistics, 1985). According to its own department of corrections report, Georgia imprisons more civilians per 100,000 population than any other political entity in the world, higher even than in the Soviet Union or South Africa.

These differences do not, as might be expected, indicate that Georgia has a more serious crime problem. In fact, its crime rates are slightly lower: the national rate is 5,800 index crimes per 100,000 inhabitants, compared with 5,625 for Georgia. The data show that sentencing is simply much harsher in Georgia—259 people per 100,000 residents are serving prison sentences, compared with 179 for the nation as a whole. If one compares Georgia with Massachusetts, for example, a state with roughly the same size resident population and crime rate, one finds that there are about 4,000 prisoners in Massachusetts, compared to about 12,000 prisoners in Georgia.

These numbers have significant implications for Georgia's IPS program. Because convicted offenders are more likely to be sentenced to prison in Georgia, its "prison-bound" offenders, as a group, probably have a lower expected risk of recidivism than those in many other states. It is a well documented fact that the length and seriousness of prior criminal record are the best predictors of recidivism. In most states, prison crowding and other considerations often result in probation sentences for younger offenders. In Georgia, offenders are more likely to be incarcerated earlier in their criminal careers and for less serious crimes. This lowers the expected recidivism rates for Georgia offenders, relative to rates in other states.

This is a critical point: if Georgia does have a pool of prison-bound offenders available who are less serious than those in other states, other states cannot expect similar results. It seems that this may be the case, given the overall recidivism rates of prisoners released in Georgia. The Georgia Office of Evaluation and Statistics reports that 30 percent of their released prisoners are reincarcerated within five years of their release; the comparable figure in California (and the nation) is about 55 percent. (Klein and Caggiano, 1986; Bureau of Justice Statistics, 1986).

By ignoring such differences, other jurisdictions may be courting disappointment and, worse, serious risks for public safety.

Putting the Program in Place

States may be in greater danger of disappointment if they do have a similar pool of offenders, and assume that this alone guarantees analogous success. Treating lower-risk offenders may be a necessary condition for the Georgia model's success, but it is not a sufficient condition. Research studies in education, urban planning, technology transfer, and criminal justice have all shown that the context and the strategies of the organization adopting an innovation are more important than the characteristics of the innovation itself for success. As noted above, Georgia's development and implementation efforts were "textbook" examples of successful adoption of innovative programs.

Jurisdictions that are considering IPS programs should be aware of the pivotal elements in program adoption, in general, and the characteristics of Georgia's effort, specifically. The pivotal elements include:

- Motivation for adoption
- Involvement of key actors
- Adaptability and communication
- Organizational resources

Motivation for Adoption. Research has found that the impetus for adopting a new program usually shapes its destiny. This is particularly true in criminal justice. Innovations that are "imposed from above" rarely achieve more than pro forma status and generally do not survive for very long. Ellickson and Petersilia (1983) found that when the "adopting" agency itself identifies or accepts the need for a program, believes that the program is in its best interests, and, especially, is willing to support or find funds for the program, success is much more likely. It is much less likely when the agency yields reluctantly to external pressure or sees the program only as an opportunity to attract extra funds.

In Georgia's case, the corrections department is the agency in question; it oversees both prison and probation, and it was strongly motivated to find an alternative to imprisonment for some of the state's felony offenders. The federal courts had threatened to take over the state's entire corrections system on the grounds of "unconstitutional" crowding. According to the Georgia Commissioner of Corrections, "the problem had reached near-catastrophic proportions...it became apparent that additional options had to be developed" (Georgia Dept. of Offender Rehabilitation, 1984: 1).

In this situation, corrections policymakers and administrators were very open to suggestions that the state consider an IPS program. It was clear that corrections could not build prisons fast enough to satisfy federal demands for reduced crowding, even if the state had the necessary funds. Corrections officials perceived that IPS might ease overcrowding by diverting some serious offenders from prison in much less time and at less cost. Consequently, they were willing to devote resources for developing and initiating the program.

In some states, this kind of response would be less likely—for political, bureaucratic, and fiscal reasons. In California, for example, prisons are operated by a state-level corrections department, but probation is the responsibility of individual counties.

Consequently, to mount IPS programs, county officials would have to use county funds, but the state would realize the benefits in reduced prison crowding. Unless some arrangement is made to reimburse the counties from state funds, they will probably not be very motivated to use scarce resources for IPS. In Georgia, probation is one agency under the administrative umbrella of a state-level corrections department. Development and operating funds for probation come from the same financial pot as funds for corrections facilities. Thus, no local jurisdiction is being asked to "give the state a handout" at county taxpayers' expense.

Involvement of Key Actors. Even where motivation is strong, an innovation will not succeed without the involvement of key actors, in and outside the adopting organization. The kind of external involvement needed will depend on the larger political and bureaucratic structure that subsumes the organization. Internally, success will depend on the organization's capacity to mobilize support from administrators, managers, and staff.

Developers of the Georgia program began by identifying key actors outside the corrections department and mobilizing their support. They realized that judicial support was the most critical to success: judges make the final sentencing decision, and if they don't believe that an IPS program meets their punitive objectives they won't sentence offenders to it.

The probation staff involved Georgia's judges in designing the IPS program, incorporating their suggestions for the program's structure and selection criteria. From the outset, it was clear the judges had to be convinced that the program would be punitive, would have a low price tag, and would not jeopardize public safety. Preliminary meetings also revealed that the judges would resist a program that reduced their discretion by forcing them to use inflexible, standardized criteria for sentencing offenders to IPS. However, the judges indicated they would agree to give IPS sentences only to offenders whose presentence investigations recommended a prison sentence. Because the probation staff took these concerns into consideration and designed the program to accommodate them, the judges have not only cooperated, but are among the program's strongest advocates.

By securing support from the governor, the probation staff also made judiciary support more secure: given the public's punitive mood, judges who give IPS sentences might seem "lenient" to their local constituents. That appearance can be mitigated if the program is approved at the highest state level. To that end, the IPS program was announced with strong approval from the governor. He followed up the announcement with a letter to the state's judges supporting IPS and urging them to sentence fewer people to prison. With that kind of backing, judges were free to try out the alternative and pass any resulting political "heat" up to the highest level.

Within the organization, IPS has had strong support from the commissioner of corrections and the probation commissioner. Conscious of political influences on program success, they have kept the public and legislators aware of the program's positive results. They also have become national spokesmen for the program, testifying frequently before Congress and professional organizations. This national visibility has fostered a sense of Georgia state pride and ownership in the program, which, in turn, has encouraged legislators to budget more funds for its expansion.

Case studies have repeatedly shown that the energy and advocacy of a single individual often make the critical difference for new programs. This person is usually a program director or "entrepreneur" who guides and mobilizes support for developing and implementing the program. Budding programs need someone to keep them alive through all the political, bureaucratic, and fiscal buffeting they undergo. Without such a person, inertia, political agendas, fiscal constraints, and distrust of an unknown will often do a program in.

Georgia's IPS program has had such a person, the probation commissioner. He championed the idea, became the program's first director, and energetically guided the conversion into practice. Continuing as director, he has established and maintained the lines of communication with other key agencies, clarified the program's goals, and encouraged staff commitment. This continuity of leadership also has been especially important for program consistency and growth.

Even if a program has all this other support going for it, it will falter without the commitment of the operational staff. Anything involving change causes stress to an organization and its staff. This is especially true when a new program involves a different "orientation." The IPS offers a cogent example. The traditional orientation of probation officers is counseling aimed at rehabilitation. An IPS program stresses surveillance, primarily for deterrence and public safety. Many probation officers simply cannot change their traditional orientation. Many also cannot adjust to being on-call 24 hours a day, working nights and weekends, and dealing with higher-risk offenders. Moving to implement IPS without considerable attention to building staff support is like "bending granite," according to the evaluator of the Massachusetts IPS program (Byrne, 1986).

Considering these natural obstacles to staff support, the Georgia program selected the probation officers for the program from experienced staff who were committed to the IPS objectives and had the skills and flexibility to change their orientation. A U.S. National Institute of Corrections grant supported extensive staff training, as well as a large public information program targeted for judges, prosecutors, and key law enforcement personnel. Program developers also involved staff in program design, particularly in deciding such things as caseload size, contact requirements, working arrangements, etc. This involvement gave the practitioners a sense of ownership and a stake in the program's success.

Adaptability and Communication. Involvement of key actors is both a purpose and a necessary condition of program adaptability and good communication. Without either, programs will be less successful—if they survive at all. From its earliest development stages, a program must adapt to the local motivations, priorities, and context. Otherwise, it becomes a procrustean bed that everyone but its strongest advocates will soon find uncomfortable.

As mentioned above, support and survival are more likely if the "model" an agency adopts can accommodate changes that will secure key actors' support. Even after a program is in place and having positive results, it must still be responsive to changes in the environment, some of which the program itself may cause. It must also respond to new ideas and better ways of doing things. None of this is possible without stable, open lines of communication. To begin with, the organization needs to establish and clearly communicate program goals and objectives. Then, it must encourage and facilitate constant interaction of all those involved.

Rather than attempting to adopt someone else's model or begin with a full-fledged program, Georgia staff began by analyzing how to make IPS work in their local context. They followed an evolutionary path, building on existing structures and prior achievements. As noted earlier, they involved judges and operational staff in developing the program, incorporating features that addressed the concerns and objectives of these key actors.

Because communication is open, staff members frequently make suggestions for change, and the program model is constantly evolving. For example, staff suggestions have led some jurisdictions to experiment with a change in caseload arrangements from 25 probationers for two officers, to 40 for three officers. Staff also suggested the need for urinalysis testing to detect drug use among IPS participants. After a pilot program, urinalysis testing was expanded and the IPS staff trained in appropriate procedures. In the interest of adaptability and communication, program administrators also routinely conduct seminars for judges, legislators, prosecutors, and key law enforcement personnel.

Organizational Resources. No matter the motivation, support of key actors, and adaptability of a program, its initiation and survival rest on an organization's financial and human resources. Adequacy of the former depends on a fortuitous combination of institutional commitment and solvency, and of the latter on the training and expertise of its staff. An organization must be prepared to make sacrifices in other areas or supplement its funds from outside sources to support an innovation. It must also invest in appropriately trained personnel from outside or in training existing staff.

The Georgia Department of Corrections recognized that intensive surveillance would cost considerably more than routine probation supervision and that the funds could not be diverted from existing operating budgets. Hence, IPS required a new source of revenue. In 1982, the probation division initiated a program to collect probation fees from their "clients." This followed a ruling by the state attorney general that such a practice would not require additional enabling legislation and that such funds could be retained for use in supervising probationers. Probation fees were imposed statewide, not exclusively on IPS probationers, but the intent was to use the additional funds to support IPS. Judges were told that establishing IPS teams in their jurisdictions would be partially dependent on their imposition of probation fees. The IPS program and the collection of supervision fees have developed and expanded simultaneously.

Giving IPS a Real Chance

It would be highly ironic if this discussion were seen as an argument against alternative sanctions to imprisonment and thus, implicitly, for constructing more prisons. Far from that, the author remains a strong advocate of alternative sanctions, especially of IPS, ''for those offenders who are too antisocial for the relative freedom that probation now offers, but not so seriously criminal as to require imprisonment'' (Petersilia, Turner and Kahan, 1985: ix). This essay springs from a concern that IPS be given the chance that so many promising criminal justice innovations have not received in the past.

The criminal justice system has been reeling from one sort of crisis to another in the years since World War II. Consequently, it has tended to see innovations as ''quick fixes'' rather than suggestive models that need time to mature and adapt to local contexts, priorities, and resources. One after another, most of these innovations have been ''tried and found wanting.'' Consider the example of halfway houses—prerelease centers for prison inmates nearing parole. Halfway houses proliferated in the early 1970s when federal funds were plentiful and a faith in the rehabilitative ideal strong. As the nation became more punitive, convinced that rehabilitation programs ''didn't work,'' halfway houses found it increasingly difficult to secure funding, began to be dismantled, and in some states, few still exist. The same is likely to happen to IPS, if other jurisdictions believe they can simply impose the Georgia model in their contexts.

The appeal is understandable: Georgia's program apparently has succeeded admirably in a very short period. Analysis of Georgia's sentencing statistics from 1982 through 1985 shows a 10 percent reduction in the proportion of convicted felons imprisoned during this time period, contrary to the nationwide trend. IPS is credited with influencing this change. Such results would certainly tempt other jurisdictions to see the model as a quick fix for their prison crowding. If they do, without considering the cautions raised in this essay, I suspect that many of them will soon face disappointing, if not downright alarming, results. In that event, Georgia's experience no doubt will be dismissed as a fluke, and IPS will join the ranks of innovations that were ''found wanting.''

The essay is also not intended to caution jurisdictions against IPS unless they can draw on a similar pool of lower-risk offenders. Rather, it is intended to argue that they should consider what their own contexts demand. What kinds of offenders do they have? How many of them could be safely supervised under the Georgia model? What kinds of procedural changes in the model would be needed to ensure public safety? These questions raise complex issues and can be answered only by a comprehensive assessment involving many actors across the system. And they are not the only questions that jurisdictions must take time to address.

Equally important questions have to do with the ways in which they can successfully adapt and implement the program, taking the nature of their ''clientele'' into consideration. The discussion of Georgia's implementation strategies is not the academic exercise that it might seem. It is also not a matter of arguing *post hoc*—that is, because Georgia succeeded, the strategies it used must have been responsible, or "nothing succeeds like success." While those strategies were largely responsible, it was only because so much analysis of so many previous case studies has pointed to these same characteristics in implementation processes that produced successful programs.

IPS may indeed be a part of, if not wholly, "the future of American corrections." But not unless jurisdictions have realistic expectations about what it can accomplish, tailor programs to fit the offenders they will treat, and understand the role that local context and adoption strategies must play.

REFERENCES

Byrne, James M. (1985). *Bending Granite: The Implementation of Intensive Probation Supervision in Massachusetts.* Paper presented at the 1985 meeting of the American Society of Criminology, San Diego, CA.

Ellickson, Phyllis and Joan Petersilia (1983). *Implementing New Ideas in Criminal Justice* [R-2929-NIJ]. Santa Monica, CA: Rand Corporation.

Erwin, Billie S. (1984). *Evaluation of Intensive Probation Supervision in Georgia.* Atlanta, GA: Dept. of Offender Rehabilitation.

———(1986a). "Turning Up the Heat on Probationers in Georgia." *Federal Probation* L:2 (June): 17-24.

———(1986b). "New Dimensions in Probation: Georgia's Experience With IPS." Unpublished draft.

Georgia Dept. of Offender Rehabilitation (1984). *Intensive Probation Supervision.*

Gettinger, Stephen (1983). "Intensive Supervision: Can It Rehabilitate Probation?" *Corrections Magazine* (April): 7-17.

Hennessey, Edward F. (1985). "Why Our Jails Are Suddenly Overcrowded." *Judges Journal* (Fall).

Klein, Stephen and Michael N. Caggiano (1986). *The Prevalence, Predictability, and Policy Implications of Recidivism* [R-3413-BJS]. Santa Monica, CA: Rand Corporation.

New York Times (1985), December 18.

Petersilia, Joan, Susan Turner and James Kahan (1985). *Granting Felons Probation: Public Risks and Alternatives* [R-3186-NIJ]. Santa Monica, CA: Rand Corporation.

U.S. Bureau of Justice Statistics (1985). *Sourcebook of Criminal Justice Statistics—1984.* Washington, DC: U.S. Government Printing Office.

———(1986) *Annual Report, Fiscal 1985.* Washington, DC: U.S. Government Printing Office.

Washington Post (1985), August 16.

Intensive Supervision in Probation: A Comparison of Three Projects

by
Todd R. Clear
Suzanne Flynn
Carol Shapiro

Intensive probation programs have become popular in the 1980s, despite the fact that there is little literature base to support them. Instead, the programs are spawned by extensive prison crowding. This paper describes intensive programs in Georgia, New Jersey and Oregon, with issues raised concerning transferability of interventions, target group specification, the emphasis on control and net widening.

Intensive supervision has taken the field of probation by storm in the middle-third of the 1980s. It seems that just about every probation agency either has an intensive program, is planning for one, or is seeking funds to implement a "new" approach to be called "intensive." The pressure for intensive probation is so widespread that no administrator can call his organization's panoply of probation methods complete without it. The chorus of approval for intensive probation is so strong and seemingly uniform that we are tempted to call it "the new panacea of corrections."

The timing of this broad-based support for a new and supposedly improved version of probation is at least ironic. Barely ten years ago, a major report by the U.S. Comptroller General concluded that state and local systems of probation were "in crisis" due to a failure either to serve the offender or to protect the public (U.S. Comptroller General, 1976). About the same time, a noted researcher had referred to one large, leading probation agency as "kind of a standing joke" (Martinson, 1976). The problems of community supervision seemed to be much larger than merely a matter of budgetary constraints, according to a federally funded report completed less than a decade ago, which found "no evidence" that smaller caseloads alone would lead to more effective supervision of adults (Banks, Porter, Rardin, Siler and Unger, 1981). This report simply repeated the findings of earlier studies (Neithercutt and Gottfredson, 1973; Carter and Wilkins, 1976). Hence, a decade ago, the idea of *more* emphasis on probation was difficult to sell, and seemed preposterous to many corrections officials and informed policymakers.

Most observers would say that during the last decade there has not been a new discovery of a probation technique that revolutionizes supervision to the degree that a revised emphasis on "intensive" probation makes sense. There has been widespread adoption of classification systems for probationers (Clear and Gallagher, 1985), and some research has suggested that both the differential supervision (Baird, Heinz and Bemus, 1977) and emphasis on detailed case planning (Lerner, Arling and Baird, 1986) that result from classification can lead to an improvement in the successfulness of supervision. Yet these studies are isolated examples in a literature that otherwise offers little hope that supervision can have a significant impact on recidivism (see, for example, Stanley, 1976; Saks and Logan, 1979; von Hirsch and Hanrahan, 1979). It requires an intellectual reach to argue that the few studies supporting intensive probation are enough to justify the great national trend toward its adoption. Indeed, perhaps the strongest recent call for more emphasis on intensive probation was contained in the discussion of findings that regular probation methods failed to control the criminal behavior of *over half* of a sample of California felons (Petersilia, Turner, Kahan and Peterson, 1985). How could more of this probation be expected reasonably to be much better?

Of course, the new call for intensive probation is not based on a firm grounding of social science. The social science base for intensive probation reform is at best only promising—and at worst downright shaky. Far from a reasoned outgrowth of a program of research and evaluation, the new movement toward intensive probation is actually a rapid response to a serious problem: system overcrowding. Nearly every jurisdiction in the United States lacks the correctional resources to carry out its promises. Intensive probation is popular largely for its perceived curative powers in regard to this problem.

However, intensive probation really poses a threat to the traditional community supervision function, for like any quick remedy, if it fails to alleviate the pain the patient will probably discard it in favor of a different medicine. It is worth noting that intensive probation is hardly a new idea. About 25 years ago, many "intensive" experiments were undertaken to determine the "best" caseload size for community supervision, despite the illogic of the proposition that a magical "best" number could be found. Nevertheless, the failure of these experiments to produce results fueled two decades' worth of cynicism about the general utility of community-based methods. When the adoption of intensive probation in the 1980s fails to cure the system's almost compulsive drive to overextend its resources, we wonder if history will be repeated, and if the recent trend toward intensive methods will be abated in the face of findings of failure.

Lest the reader get the wrong impression, the authors of this paper are strong supporters of community corrections and see much value in the idea of intensive supervision. Our fear is that it is easy to lose sight of what a simple mechanism—supervision—can realistically mean to both offenders and the system. As is true for any potentially successful program (Twain, 1983), an unthinking adoption of the intensive approach can ultimately fail and leave a probation agency in a worse circumstance than existed prior to its adoption. By raising a few questions about the use of intensive methods, we hope to promote a critical understanding of the role of probation, especially as used intensively.

The purpose of this paper is to describe three popular intensive probation programs, and to use these descriptions as a springboard for a critical appraisal of the "intensive" concept. We are not critical of these programs, per se. Each makes a contribution to its jurisdiction; each provides us with a better understanding of the role of probation as a part of the correctional process. However, the vast differences between the programs, as well as specific problems which they currently confront, help to underscore a set of issues about intensive probation, with which we conclude the paper.

THE INTENSIVE PROBATION PROGRAMS

The descriptions that follow are not complete accounts of the intensive programs—it would be impossible to provide truly complete assessments of any program as complex as intensive supervision. Instead, these descriptions highlight certain aspects of each program in order to provide a basis for raising a series of questions about the general concepts underlying these programs. The descriptions are based on published documents (Administrative Office, 1984; Erwin, 1984; Erwin and Clear, 1985; Clear and Shapiro, 1986) as well as personal involvement (one author serves on the advisory board of one project and has been instrumental in the design and evolution of a second project, while the three authors have collaborated to implement the third project).

Georgia's Intensive Probation Supervision (IPS) Project

During the late 1970s the Georgia Department of Offender Rehabilitation (now the Department of Corrections) experimented with a series of intensive supervision efforts which led, in the 1980s, to the initiation of 26 pilot intensive supervision caseloads. The project, which is operated by a statewide agency under the executive branch of government, has since grown to cover the entire State of Georgia.

The program was designed to respond to extreme levels of institutional crowding in Georgia's prisons, and the hope was eventually to enlarge the program's capacity to supervise 1,000 offenders or more at a time. This was seen as enabling Georgia to avoid the construction costs of up to two prisons. In its short time of operation, nearly 2,000 offenders have been processed under the program. By the account of most observers, inside Georgia and out, the program has enjoyed considerable success and is widely supported and respected.

Staff for the program was drawn from existing officers in the system and from other law enforcement agencies. Among those who volunteered, the most promising were selected. In conversation with IPS officers it is easy to become impressed with their optimism and enthusiasm for the job, and this sets them apart in tone from staffs in many other probation agencies around the country. Perhaps one of the reasons IPS staffers seem more energetic is that extensive training has been provided to them in support of their work. In addition, while the central office in Atlanta maintains a careful interest, field staff are given a reasonable degree of latitude to implement the IPS program in ways that fit the idiosyncrasies of local courts.

Georgia's IPS program is deliberately strict, at least on paper. Caseloads not to exceed 25 offenders are handled by a two-person team: a probation officer and a surveillance officer. It was intended that the probation officer would serve as a caseworker, providing either direct services or access to social services based on the client's particular needs, while the surveillance officer would be responsible for monitoring the probationer's conduct and compliance with IPS conditions. In practice, these roles have blended. Because the surveillance officer frequently visits the client in the home, he is faced with numerous opportunities to provide services to the probationer and the client's family. In contrast, it is the probation officer who ultimately takes responsibility for enforcing IPS conditions by revoking probation, should this become necessary. Therefore, no clear role differentiation has occurred, and most IPS teams agree that their jobs are not highly specialized.

Double-teaming was presumed necessary because of the rather extensive requirements placed on the IPS client: community service, restitution, employment, curfew, and frequent and random urine checks are standard requirements, to which the probation officer may add drug or alcohol treatment, mental health treatment and other special conditions. These conditions are enforced by very frequent contact—up to twice daily during the first weeks of supervision, and then daily, at least for the initial months of supervision.

Selection of IPS clients occurs in two ways. In some counties, IPS teams review all cases sentenced to prison (excluding violent offenders) for good IPS candidates, and then petition the judge for resentencing the offender if the team finds the case appropriate for IPS (a decision which may be based only on the presentence report, but usually includes an interview of the client, as well). In other counties, judges are allowed to sentence directly to IPS, should the IPS team deem the client appropriate. The IPS can recommend intensive probation as an alternative if a prison sentence would otherwise have been recommended in the presentence report. Whichever procedure is used, the judge is required to sign a statement saying that without IPS the defendant would have been given an incarcerative term.

Despite these safeguards, Georgia Department of Corrections' (DOC) evaluations show that IPS cases look, on the whole, very similar to regular probation cases in Georgia, particularly when it comes to the risk of new criminal behavior. IPS cases have somewhat more serious criminal records, including the current offense, and discriminant function analyses have suggested that as many as half the IPS cases may be true diversions from prison. Nevertheless, a profile of IPS clients is not much different from a profile of regular probation cases (statewide), yet is remarkably dissimilar from a profile of imprisoned offenders. In addition, over half of the IPS cases fall into the two lowest risk categories (out of four) of Georgia's risk assessment instrument.

Apparently, then, Georgia's IPS, which constitutes a significantly enhanced level of supervision over regular probation (a client-staff ratio of 12.5:1 compared to a common statewide ratio of 120:1 or greater), is applied to a population not markedly different from the regular probation population. How can this be true, when the IPS selection process is so deliberate and the true diversion rate is so high?

The answer to this question may lie in a broader understanding of Georgia's punishment process. According to the U.S. Bureau of Justice Statistics (1983), Georgia ranks in the top five states in both incarceration rate and probation rate. This means that while there are many candidates for IPS in Georgia among those going to prison, the prison-bound Georgia offenders include many who quite reasonably might have been assigned to probation, which is also a heavily used correctional method. Thus, it is easy to imagine that many of the less serious prison-bound cases look a good deal like numerous cases already on probation. It may be that IPS keeps those cases.

Georgia's IPS has continued to enjoy strong support from both the legislative and judicial branches of government. According to the officials who designed and administer IPS, the "tough and strict" rhetoric of the program, combined with a purposeful program of publicity with the media and key government officials, has helped to sustain support for the community-based program in an otherwise conservative jurisdiction.

Recent results of the program are not likely to damage that support. The first 1,000 offenders placed in the program committed barely over 100 crimes in their first 18 months under supervision, and only a handful of these crimes were serious felonies (such as robbery, burglary and rape). We are left with the distinct impression that Georgia could probably triple the size of its program with little or no change in overall levels of public safety.

New Jersey's Intensive Supervision Program (ISP)

The Intensive Supervision Program in New Jersey resulted from a one year effort (in 1982-3) of the Administrative Office of the Courts (AOC) to develop a set of Administrative Rules of Probation to guide the practices of 21 county probation departments organized into (then) 18 judicial vicinages. Because probation in New Jersey is funded, staffed and administered at the county (or vicinage) level, the AOC had for several years been struggling to establish greater authority over the diverse practices of probation in these local, semiautonomous units. In this process, ISP was an idea developed by one subcommittee charged with demonstrating probation's potential as an effective alternative to sentences to overcrowded prisons.

The ISP became the first (and thus far the only) direct client-service program run from the AOC. As such, it is not only a highly visible program within the state, but it is the first attempt of the AOC to demonstrate to the localities how a centrally administered line operation program might work. Its manifest goal is to supervise "one prison's worth of offenders (about 500)" on the street. Its latent goal is to establish the AOC's competence in direct administration of probation services. Thus, ISP has nearly as much symbolic importance in New Jersey as it has practical potential for dealing with the state's serious prison crowding problem.

Probation officers were selected via a series of extensive interviews and tests of volunteers from existing staff. Once selected, each ISP officer received an immediate raise in pay, and was assigned to attend extensive training in the methods of intensive supervision.

The tenets of the ISP are a mix of tough talk and client support. All clients must have a job. Community service, restitution and a curfew are almost always conditions of ISP, as are alcohol, drug and/or mental health treatment. On the other hand, prior to acceptance into the program, every client must write a "plan" outlining his or her actions to deal with whatever "problems" interfere with the client's normal, productive functioning. Each client must also keep a daily diary that serves as a basis for discussing how a client is adjusting to the intensive program. In order to have sufficient time to enforce these requirements, each officer is limited to 25 cases, and each case must be seen weekly or more, depending on the client's status in the program. By all accounts, officers consistently achieve contact requirements.

ISP officials are proud to point out that theirs is a 24 hour, 7-day-a-week program. Officers work nights and weekends on a regular basis, and are on call at all times. While many ISP officers complain that the schedule leads to burnout, they also give the impression that they respect the close level of supervision they can give, feel they are doing "real probation," and enjoy their prestige as the "elite" of the state's probation workers.

It took nearly a year for the ISP program to reach full speed because the rate of acceptance of offenders into the program was both low and slow. The screening process probably accounts for this delay. Within 30 days of the sentence to prison, any offender who meets the statutory criteria may apply in writing for ISP consideration. (Most people convicted of violent crimes are excluded from consideration, as are some other serious offenders. The application packet, which includes the offender's community plan, is forwarded to a panel composed of a retired judge, a retired correction official and a chief justice appointee. If the panel finds the offender acceptable, it recommends to the original sentencing judge that his order be amended to assign the offender to ISP. If the judge agrees (which usually happens, since the chief justice supports the program and wields extensive influence on the judiciary), the offender is released into ISP. This elaborate procedure is designed to promote quality control in selection of ISP cases, while also avoiding net-widening, but it has resulted in a slow trickle of cases into the program.

Jackson Toby and Frank Pearson of Rutgers University are currently completing an evaluation of New Jersey's ISP, and therefore it is too early to provide conclusive data on the program's effectiveness. Some preliminary data released by the AOC (Goldstein, 1986) seem to suggest directions which that evaluation may take, however. Only about 80 percent of the ISP clients appear to make it past the first six months; most who fail do so because of non-compliance with the program's requirements rather than new crimes. While the ISP caseloads contain several clients with serious criminal backgrounds, the majority are drug offenders (including many possession cases, but some burglary cases).

Some observers have questioned whether the screening process is too stringent, resulting in ISP cases that do not really "need" strict, close supervision. Certainly, ISP clients, while clearly prison-bound in every case, do not appear to be the most serious or high risk offenders. The irony is that while this mid-to-low range client enters a carefully structured program as one of an officer's 25 cases, with much less planning the far higher risk regular parolee joins a caseload in excess of 100 cases. To this problem must be added a growing concern that some judges are "backdooring" cases into ISP by sentencing borderline offenders to prison while announcing they will "welcome an application for intensive supervision." Yet, whether the borderline case will be approved by the panel for resentencing remains an open question.

Despite these problems, ISP in New Jersey is a widely acclaimed program. There is some complaint from prosecutors and isolated elected officials, but to date this seems far outweighed by strong judicial support for the program, coupled with very complimentary media coverage and acceptance by criminal justice officials and the chief executive. Prison crowding is considered too serious to allow destruction of the program.

Multnomah County, Oregon's Probation Development Project (PDP)

For a decade, the Edna McConnell-Clark Foundation has been interested in funding programs leading to increased use of alternatives to incarceration. Recently, a grant was given to the Program Resources Center of Rutgers University to conduct an organizational development project in probation, and the site selected was Multnomah County (Portland), Oregon.

Because Oregon is a community corrections state, the administrative structure of the PDP involves a three-way agreement between the Rutgers center, the state department of corrections and the Justice Services Department of Multnomah County. The two Oregon agencies provide staff and material support, while the Rutgers center provides research, consultation and financial support.

The purpose of the PDP is to provide enhanced probation supervision to 100-150 incarceration-bound offenders each year. Two forces in Oregon make the PDP a particularly useful demonstration project for community corrections in that state. First, there is severe crowding: prisons are operating at 130 percent capacity, and jails are similarly strained. The second factor is the Oregon Community Corrections Act—the reimbursement provisions of the law provide a financial advantage for Multnomah County to keep certain felons in the community. Because of these two forces, a strong incentive exists to avoid incarcerative sentences.

The PDP is not purely an "intensive supervision" project; it is actually an organizational development demonstration project. The intensive supervision method is a way of demonstrating the potential of probation with incarceration-bound offenders, but the main focus is organization development. The project operates with a Probation Task Force made up of probation officers who assist in the operational decision-making. This group has conducted management audits and other organizational studies in order to develop the design of the PDP unit, which carries out the supervision of offenders. There is also a PDP Community Advisory Board, which establishes project policy. This 16-member group is made up of citizens, criminal justice leaders, and elected government officials.

The project-development work of the task force and advisory board lasted 18 months before the first offender was brought under supervision by the PDP. During that time, two research studies were completed, one to develop and validate a risk screening device, the other to analyze sentencing patterns. Extensive training was conducted for the probation department, the PDP unit (selected from among volunteers), the task force and the advisory board. Several policy papers were written, and three project retreats were held.

The result of this process was the careful delineation of project policies and the identification of a target group for supervision. Supervision policies emphasize enforcement of a streamlined set of supervision conditions. Rather than the "get tough" model of intensive supervision, the PDP seeks to identify only one or two special conditions that relate to the specific factors in the client's life that produce a risk for the community, and the one or two punitive conditions that demonstrate to the offender the seriousness of the offense. Each offender's conditions are a limited number of targeted, individualized requirements that are demonstrably related to the offense and the offender's background. Emphasis also is placed on differentiating supervision rules that are primarily punitive in nature from those designed to control risk. Although there are fewer, often less restrictive conditions applied to PDP cases, they are to be strictly enforced. The philosophy of the PDP is that too much has been promised by probation (often in the form of multiple conditions) and too often probation fails to deliver on these promises. By promising less, and consistently performing as promised, it is hoped that PDP will increase the credibility of probation as an alternative.

The PDP offender target group was identified by research on prior sentencing practices. It was learned that over 85 percent of all low risk offenders already receive probation terms in Multnomah County regardless of crime seriousness, and about half of the moderate to high risk/moderate crime seriousness cases receive such sentences. Only the high risk, serious criminal offender is truly "incarceration-bound."

Therefore, the PDP refuses to consider any low risk offender, regardless of the circumstances of the case. By advisory board policy, high risk and high crime seriousness cases also are excluded. Thus, the target population includes moderate crime seriousness cases representing moderate or high risk to the community. These are the borderline cases that so often trouble the criminal justice system—the crime is not so serious to demand incarceration, but the offender's risk makes traditional supervision problematic. Among offenders who fit this category, the PDP unit considers only those whose presentence recommendation includes prison time or jail time in excess of 90 days. These incarceration-bound offenders are interviewed by the PDP team, and an extensive case plan is developed by the team. When the plan is believed acceptable to the unit, an alternative recommendation is drawn up to accompany the presentence report. Should the judge agree with the PDP assessment (which is presented by a unit member in court), the client is sentenced to this option. No direct sentencing to the PDP can occur without the unit's recommendation.

The case assessment process and the design of the case plan are fraught with discretion. Guidelines for case assessment, recommendations, supervision methods and contact requirements are fairly broad, and specific decisions are left to the judgment of the PDP team. Rather than strict, intensive supervision, the emphasis of the PDP is on careful assessment and planning of cases: this normally results in intensive supervision—at least weekly contact.

It is too early to evaluate the effectiveness of the PDP. After three months of receiving cases, it is clear that there are numerous moderate risk cases that can be accepted to the PDP. In Multnomah County, approximately one case per day fits the PDP unit's eligibility requirements and is scheduled for an interview. About one-half of the offenders interviewed are recommended for the PDP unit. Judges follow this recommendation about two-thirds of the time.

However, because the project is externally funded, and is not an initiative of any of the criminal justice agencies in Multnomah County, it occupies a precarious position in the system's priorities. Justice officials have been supportive of the idea, but maintain a note of caution about probation's ability to provide the necessary supervision and services. The project strategy has been carefully designed to transfer control of the project from the three-party agreement to the local justice officials, but the permanence of the PDP will probably depend on its performance as an alternative to prison, as well as the unpredictable events that occur in the political context of the project.

PATTERNS IN THE USE OF INTENSIVE SUPERVISION

These three programs illustrate some of the common patterns that emerge in the new intensive supervision movement in probation. First and foremost, these programs base their existence on a rationale linked to the problem of institutional crowding. Traditional probation is not seen as a suitable alternative to incarceration for the prison-bound offender, and so a "new improved" probation is needed if community supervision is to be useful in ameliorating the crowding problem. In this way, intensive supervision stands as a subtle, implied criticism that traditional probation is not capable of handling the system's needs for supervision of serious offenders.

In order to meet these needs, the intensive version of probation provides a "get-tough" and strict rationale. Intrusive conditions—both those related to risk and those that are primarily punitive—are commonplace, and the rhetoric emphasizes enforcement. Because these programs are designed to deal with an incarcerated subpopulation of offenders, they must advertise a difference in approach; they must establish themselves as a contrast to "slap-on-the-wrist" probation. The best way to do this is through visibly stern conditions and an emphasis on enforcement, and this has been the general strategy of intensive programs.

In order to make them "special," the intensive programs typically are set apart from traditional probation. Officers with an intensive supervision caseload normally find themselves in a separate reporting structure in the organization, not subject to the same hierarchical patterns or personalities that operate for traditional supervision. This has the effect of highlighting the intensive function, and it often receives special treatment both in resources and in personnel practices. The result is often a high-profile, high-morale subsection of an organization's larger operations. This suboperation is often perceived by those who are not a part of it as receiving a disproportionate share of resources to manage a group of "hand-picked clients," at the expense of the rest of the organization. Therefore, there is normally strong pressure on the intensive program to demonstrate results.

This is one reason why these programs often seem to be encased in an atmosphere of caution—they are very vulnerable to errors. Based on a rationale of effective offender control, and in contrast to seemingly more lenient traditional probation methods, the idea of intensive probation can be seriously damaged by even one publicized incident of serious client failure, such as a violent crime. Therefore, despite the control rhetoric, program officials seem to bend over backwards to avoid the riskiest clients and to resist giving accepted clients many chances to violate probation. Borderline cases are often rejected, at least in the early stages of most programs.

Thus, intensive programs such as the three described here seem to share several characteristics. First, their lifeblood is extensive institutional crowding in the corrections system. Second, they are high-profile, specialized programs that have been differentiated from traditional supervision practices both structurally and conceptually. Third, they tend to be cautious in accepting clients. Fourth, their programmatic thrust is an emphasis on control and strict accountability.

These shared characteristics should not be allowed to obscure several differences among the programs. The most common programmatic difference is organizational context. Some programs' governmental location is judicial, others are housed with the county executive, still others are run by the state executive. Some projects are small experiments, others are large, seemingly long-term program initiatives. In practice, the actions of intensive officers vary widely. Some officers are provided a great deal of discretion in planning and conducting supervision, other officers' decisions are tightly controlled by elaborate program requirements. Moreover, the amount of supervision that is called "intensive" varies widely, from twice-monthly contact to at least daily contact (Baird, 1984).

FOUR ISSUES IN INTENSIVE SUPERVISION PROGRAMS

We are left with a sense of unease about the use of intensive probation. The similarities and differences described above seem to be interwoven with a theme of convenience that sometimes borders on expediency. Intensive programs are rapidly designed responses to very serious system problems, and we wonder how well program advocates have thought through the implications of their work. The four issues below summarize our concerns about the new proliferation of intensive programs.

Transferability of Interventions

There seems to be a prevailing opinion in the probation field that once a program is shown to be "successful" somewhere, it can be transferred easily to other settings. Thus, a significant percentage of the administrators' time in Georgia and New Jersey is spent hosting visitors from other states and even other nations who want to learn about the program and decide whether to adopt it in their own jurisdictions. This thinking is a bit naive— programs work because they fit their specific contexts, not because they are sure-fire ways to solve the overall problem. The evaluation literature is full of examples of programs that were effective in one setting, but failed in others (Martinson, 1974; Palmer, 1975; Twain, 1983).

A comparison of Georgia and Oregon illustrates this point. These jurisdictions have basic differences in existing sentencing policies. In Georgia, there are high rates of incarceration and probation sentences. The result is that many offenders are incarcerated who fall into the lower risk, lower crime seriousness ranges of offenders. In Multnomah County, by contrast, the vast majority of low risk offenders are already placed on probation, as are the majority of moderate risk offenders, even when crime seriousness is taken into account. The pool of low risk, incarceration-bound offenders that exists in Georgia simply does not exist in any meaningful size in Multnomah County. Over 80 percent of Multnomah County's felons are sentenced to probation.

In addition, Multnomah County judges often sentence offenders to local jail time because it is a more severe sentence than a prison term. In fact, due to good time and release policies, a prisoner sentenced to a one year jail term will, on the average, serve more time than a person sentenced to a short term in the state's prison system. This is not generally the case in Georgia, where prison terms are more severe than jail terms.

For these reasons, the offender selection program used in Georgia would probably not work in Multnomah County. If the latter project allowed low risk offenders to be placed under supervision, this would lead to eligibility for a large number of offenders who would probably receive probation terms anyway. However, the lack of such restrictions in Georgia enables IPS workers there to consider a reasonably large pool of low risk offenders who might otherwise be prison-bound. Similarly, Georgia's focus on prison-bound offenders makes sense in light of its imprisonment rate, but the extensive use of jail in Multnomah County justifies the inclusion of some jail cases as eligibles.

To simply borrow one version of intensive supervision and transfer it to a different jurisdiction may not work. In order to make an intensive supervision program effective, an analysis must be conducted of the justice system processes within which the supervision program will operate. It is most important to get a good idea of the type of offender the program is being designed to supervise. This requires an assessment of current sentencing practices and the development of a selection process that can work within existing practices.

In order to be effective, an intensive supervision project needs to emphasize *process* as much as, if not more than, program elements. Basic research needs to be conducted to determine the best target group for the project, and a detailed understanding of current justice system practices is needed to determine the best selection process to get the target group into the intensive program. The question is not whether a given intensive model is "best," but what elements of that model might work well in another setting.

The Target Group

One of the ironies of intensive supervision programs is that they represent a grand escalation of the community supervision function that is often applied to a relatively low risk population. While a subpopulation of incarceration-bound offenders can rightfully be thought to represent some risk to the community, the correctional resource question is one of relative risk: What risk level is represented by intensive supervision clients compared to other offenders in the corrections system?

A rational risk-management process would mean that the most restrictive correctional methods are applied to the highest risk clients in the system. Clients who represent lower risk would receive relatively less restrictive correctional measures. As higher risk offenders remain crime-free, they are moved to less restrictive settings (O'Leary and Clear, 1984).

Most intensive supervision programs have been directed toward offenders in such a way that rational risk management does not occur. For example, New Jersey's ISP takes only the best risks from among those sentenced to prison, and places them in caseloads of 25. Clients are seen at least twice weekly, in some cases daily. Money is available for contractual services. Most aspects of the clients' lives are closely monitored, including compliance with a strict curfew. Recently, electronic surveillance bracelets have been required for many of these clients. At the other end of the corrections process, the clients classified as too great a risk to be considered for ISP are eventually released to regular parole. Caseloads are 100 or more, there is virtually no money for contractual services and there is little capacity to monitor compliance with conditions. Many of these offenders are not even seen monthly.

The situation in Georgia is similar. Georgia's IPS cases look more similar to regular probationers than to prisoners. Yet they receive the most powerful supervision Georgia corrections can provide. Two questions arise: Why is this level of control appropriate for ISP cases, but not for regular probation cases, even though they look so similar? If this supervision is necessary for IPS cases, then why not for the released prison population in Georgia, who score much higher on risk factors?

Logical as this argument may seem, it fails in most states due to political considerations. The intensive programs are designed as politically palatable ways of responding to serious crowding. If any group of offenders is to be selected from among those creating the crowding problem, of course it will be those representing the least risk to the community. The fact that almost all offenders, including the most risky, eventually end up in the community has not been persuasive in getting budgetmakers to improve the risk-management capacity of the agencies dealing with these offenders. The primary goal of the new intensive programs is clearly to cover for a corrections system strapped for resources. That the use of these programs results in an irrational allocation of risk-control resources is a commentary on the fragmentation and goal displacement throughout correctional work.

A Programmatic Emphasis on Control

A case can be made that the majority of intensive supervision clients would do well with very little or no supervision. Instead, the intensive model incorporates the most aggressive control mechanisms in the community supervision arsenal, and as these programs age they seem to add to rather than reduce their control methods.

Many free citizens would have trouble surviving the level of supervision that occurs in Georgia. Sometimes more than daily contact, surprise home visits, curfews, weekly urine tests — how many of us would be found engaging in some misconduct if we were subjected to this regimen for six months or more?

The emphasis on control is problematic on three grounds. First, the rhetoric of control is really a type of public promise by the corrections system — serious offenders will not be coddled, they will be controlled. Yet the supervision methods are so effective that they inevitably turn up frequent misconduct that is inconsequential to public safety, but is misconduct just the same. After the big promise of enforcement, what is the intensive officer to do? A violation often requires a far more severe response than regular probationers would receive, but to do nothing is to expose the guarantees of the intensive model as hollow.

A second problem occurs when the emphasis on surveillance and control is out of proportion to the real need of the probationer for services and support. While the Georgia experience has shown that the roles of control and assistance are much more complementary in practice than many critics suggest, it is still the case that the probation officer is a finite resource of time and attention. Each minute that is spent solely on control is a minute that is not available for assistance-related tasks. No matter how much these functions may be compatible, they are not identical. To the degree that intensive methods give priority to control, treatment takes a secondary place. Because of the screening methods employed by many of these programs, the clients are often compulsive offenders whose drug and alcohol histories suggest that some form of treatment may be as important to long-term adjustment as is control. Since even in the most ambitious supervision efforts the probation officer is with the client no more than three hours a week, or less than 3 percent of the client's waking moments, something more than mere surveillance seems called for.

The third problem has already been mentioned: this heavy emphasis on control seems wasted on the wrong group. Georgia's IPS offenders produced barely more than one arrest per ten clients in an 18-month period; New Jersey's results were similar. The surveillance ammunition seems misdirected when one sees that rates of new crimes among regular parolees and probationers in both states run as high or higher than those of intensive clients.

It must be recognized that the emphasis on control was not promoted because of the specific characteristics of the clients. Requirements in most IPS programs were determined before the first offender was accepted for supervision. Instead, the supervision program is more of a public relations gesture designed to avoid criticism from a skeptical public. The fact that the eventual intensive programs are very cautious in accepting clients seems not to produce a reduction in intrusiveness of program requirements.

The Net of Social Control

It is now a familiar argument that too many so-called alternatives to incarceration inadvertently result in a larger net of social control (Krisberg and Austin, 1980). It is ironic that these intensive programs, though designed to overcome crowding problems, may actually backfire, resulting in an increase in incarceration prison-days in a given jurisdiction.

Oregon provides an excellent example of how this net enlargement might occur. The offenders eligible for this project look a great deal like other middle to high risk cases that are on probation. These offenders are about to be sentenced to incarcerative terms; in some cases the recommended terms are 90-180 days in jail. Through the intervention of the PDP team, the person is allowed "a chance" to function in the community under close control. When such a person, given a "break," fails under the terms of intensive probation, the temptation is to respond with an even harsher term than was originally intended. After all, the offender is a double failure. Not only did he or she commit the original offense, but this was followed by an uncooperative response to the "break" the system offered. This was the rationale used by a judge to impose a five year prison term on the PDP's first revocation, even though the revocation was for technical reasons (failure to attend treatment) and the original sentence recommendation was only one year.

This is different problem from the usual form of "net-widening." Normally, this criticism of alternatives means that they are applied to a group of offenders who would otherwise not be given such a severe alternative. There is a good evidence the three programs described here avoid that traditional type of net-widening. New Jersey selects only offenders already incarcerated. Studies show that the majority of Georgia and Oregon offenders would have been incarcerated without the intensive alternative. These programs appear to tap an incarceration-bound population that can be kept in the community under highly visible, enhanced controls.

Exposed to intensive controls in the community, many probationers fail. More often than not, the failure is not a new crime, but the probationer's inability to live under the escalated controls of intensive supervision. Then the system must respond, if only to retain some measure of credibility. Frequently, the response is far more severe than the original sentence from which the offender was diverted.

The mathematics of net widening is easy to estimate. If about one-half of the intensive clients are true diversions, and one-third of those fail, and the failures receive sanctions double the original term or longer, then the actual savings in person-incarceration days are negligible. The original aim of making a dent in prison crowding is lost in the face of secondary objectives of appearing tough on crime and misconduct.

DISCUSSION

Applied with careful planning and attention to potential problems, intensive supervision can be a valuable approach in community corrections. Without careful planning and consideration of serious issues, there is a real potential that programs will exacerbate the very problems they are designed to solve. There are four particular difficulties.

First, the intensive approach is best designed for moderate to high risk offenders instead of the lower risk clients these programs often deal with. Second, the promises made for intensive programs — in terms of financial conditions, punitive conditions and compliance with treatment — are difficult to achieve and may be irrelevant to the situations of many intensive clients. A far better approach is to de-escalate the conditions applied to all clients, including intensive supervision, regular supervision and even incarcerated clients.

For intensive programs, a panorama of probation conditions is probably inappropriate. Instead, an individualized set of limits should be developed that reflects a community-based approach to the seriousness of the offender's crime and the risk the offender represents. Doing more than this may be good public relations, but it is probably bad public policy.

Third, there has been a failure to clarify the differences between the goals of reducing overcrowding and increasing offender reintegration. They require different processes, and a program which attempts to achieve one may not necessarily achieve the other.

The final culprit is the panacea phenomenon in corrections. We do not believe that intensive supervision is a good idea in and of itself. Indeed, there is a large body of research and observation suggesting that past intensive methods have been at best ineffective, at worst counterproductive. Unless correctional leaders are willing to face up to their obligation to improve past performance through careful planning and implementation of the 1980s version of intensive methods (instead of the all too common unthinking adoption of the hottest new idea), those failures are bound to be repeated.

REFERENCES

Administrative Office of the Courts of New Jersey (1984). *Manual for the Intensive Supervision Program*. Trenton: Administrative Office of the Courts.

Baird, S. Christopher (1984). *Intensive Supervision in Probation*. Washington, DC: U.S. National Institute of Corrections. Mimeo.

——, Richard C. Heinz and Brian J. Bemus (1977). *The Wisconsin Classification and Workload Project, Report #2*. Madison: Bureau of Correctional Services. Mimeo.

Banks, J., A.L. Porter, R.L. Rardin, T. R. Siler and V.E. Unger (1981). *Phase I Evaluation of Intensive Special Probation Projects:* Washington, DC: U.S.

Department of Justice.

Carter, Robert M. and Leslie T. Wilkins (1976). "Caseloads: Some Conceptual Models." In *Probation, Parole and Community Corrections*, edited by Robert M. Carter and Leslie T. Wilkins. 2nd ed. New York: Wiley.

Clear, Todd R. and Kenneth W. Gallagher (1985). "Probation and Parole Supervision: A Review of Current Classification Practices." *Crime & Delinquency* 31:3 (Summer): 423.

———and Carol Shapiro (1986). "Identifying High Risk Probationers for Community Supervision." *Federal Probation* 40:2 (Spring):42-50.

Erwin, Billie S. (1984). "Evaluation of Intensive Probation Supervision in Georgia." Atlanta: Dept. of Offender Rehabilitation. Mimeo.

———, and Todd R. Clear (1985). "The Conflict Between Service and Surveillance in Supervision: The Georgia Experience." Paper presented to the American Society of Criminology, San Diego, CA (November).

Goldstein, Harvey (1986). "Intensive Supervision in New Jersey Probation." Speech presented to the Second Annual Conference of the New Jersey Criminal Deportation Commission (May 20).

Krisberg, Barry and James Austin (1980). *The Unmet Promise of Alternatives to Incarceration*. San Francisco: National Council on Crime and Delinquency. Mimeo.

Lerner, Kenneth, Gary Arling and S. Christopher Baird (1986). "Client Management Classification: Strategies for Case Supervision." *Crime & Delinquency* 32:3 (Summer): 254-271.

Martinson, Robert (1974). "What Works?--Questions and Answers About Prison Reform." *Public Interest* 35:2 (Spring): 22.

———(1976). "California Research at the Crossroads." *Crime & Delinquency* 23:2 (Spring): 180.

Neithercutt, M. and D.M. Gottfredson (1973). *Caseload Size Variation and Difference in Probation/Parole Performance*. Washington, DC: U.S. National Institute of Juvenile Justice.

O'Leary, Vincent and Todd R. Clear (1984). *Community Corrections in the 1990s*. Washington, DC: U.S. National Institute of Corrections.

Palmer, Ted (1975). "Martinson Revisited." *Journal of Research in Crime and Delinquency* 12:2 (Spring): 230.

Petersilia, Joan, Susan Turner, James Kahan and Joyce Peterson (1985). *Granting Felons Probation: Public Risks and Alternatives*. Santa Monica, CA: Rand Corporation.

Saks, Howard R. and Charles H. Logan (1979). *Does Parole Make a (Lasting) Difference?* West Hartford: University of Connecticut School of Law.

Stanley, David T. (1976). *Prisoners Among Us: The Problem of Parole*. Washington, DC: Brookings Institution.

Twain, David (1983). *Creating Change in Social Settings: Planned Program*

Development. New York: Praeger.

U.S. Bureau of Justice Statistics (1983). *Report to the Nation on Crime and Justice.* Washington, DC: U.S. Dept. of Justice.

U.S. Comptroller General (1976). *State and County Probation: Systems in Crisis.* Washington, DC: U.S. Government Printing Office.

von Hirsch, Andrew and Kathleen Hanrahan (1979). *The Question of Parole: Retention, Reform or Abolition?* Cambridge, MA: Ballinger.

Managing Change in Probation: Principles and Practice in the Implementation of an Intensive Probation Supervision Program

by
Ronald P. Corbett, Jr.
Donald Cochran
James M. Byrne

Innovations in criminal justice are rarely informed by theory or research developed in an academic setting. Similarly, academics rarely consult practitioners. This failure to collaborate impoverishes both practical and theoretical work in criminal justice. A case study of organizational change in a state probation agency serves as a context for the interweaving of practical and academic perspectives. A variety of theoretical work from several disciplines is drawn upon in developing principles for successful change efforts within organizations.

Public Service is a great dinosaur slowly moving forward. You jump on its tail to get a message sent to the brain. If you want it to turn around,

it gets all confused. The right feet start moving; the left feet remain fixed.
                                    Rep. Barney Frank (D-Mass.) in 1972,
                          regarding the task of changing bureaucracies

INTRODUCTION

The criminal justice world—comprised of academics and practitioners—
is profoundly segregated. Practitioners rarely talk to or work with those
who teach and write about criminal justice. Similarly, academics rarely
confer with or consult the practitioners. Consequently, practice is rarely
informed by solid theory and research, while academic work often lags
behind practice and lacks a real world flavor. Bennis, Benne, Chin and
Corey (1976: 4) make this point in the introduction to the revised edition
of their well known text on planned change: "We have developed a
substantial body of theory and certainly a rich body of practice, but
somehow our failure has been to provide the necessary transformation
and bridgings between the two."

This paper is principally an effort to bridge that gap in the context of
innovation and planned (and not-so-planned) change. The following is an
attempt to set out some principles for achieving success (or avoiding dismal
failure) when undertaking change in a bureaucracy. It does not represent
an attempt to construct a model for change (indeed, the idea of "models"
will be criticized), but rather to enunciate certain principles which com-
mend themselves to consideration wherever change is to be undertaken.
The discussion of these principles, however, will be joined with observations as to their impact in practice. The goal is to examine research and
literature on change in the context of an actual case study of change. The
case study involves an effort by the Massachusetts Probation Agency to
implement an Intensive Probation Supervision (IPS) program. The material
for the paper was gathered in conjunction with a federally funded evaluation study, and included interviews, on-site observations, performance
monitoring, data collection and analysis. Fifteen sites and approximately
150 personnel were involved in the study. The voices of both the
academics and practitioners will be heard in this paper: it will be maintained that only when the two are merged, and the resultant synergy takes
place, that successful efforts at change can be made.

THE ACADEMIC/PRACTITIONER CONNECTION

This interweaving of academic and practical perspectives, while generally rare in criminal justice, is indicative of a shift that commenced nearly

a year before the IPS Program was implemented in Massachusetts. A newly appointed (1984) agency head established linkages with the academic world in the following specific ways:

• By contracting with a local private university for technical assistance in computer training for probation managers as well as statistical research on the case classification system.

• By jointly obtaining a foundation grant with a second local private university to develop "games" or "simulations" in mediation and conflict resolution techniques. These games or simulations are then to be used to train probation officers.

• By contracting with a third local private university to run a series of seminars entitled "The Humanities and the Profession," in which selected probation personnel were sent jointly selected literary pieces (short stories, plays, and novels) and then invited to participate with their colleagues in on-campus, faculty-led discussions of professional and ethical issues raised in the texts.

• By forming a citizen advisory board, comprised in part of three faculty members from local state and private universities.

• And, most pertinently, by becoming a co-applicant with a state university on the grant that funded the experimental IPS program and the related research effort.

BACKGROUND TO CHANGE

David Twain (1983: 33) offers a concise rationale for placing any reform effort in its proper historical/cultural context: "There are traditions that influence the transactions in a community. The rationale for community practices must be understood and the power of traditions respected if necessary and successful change is to be accomplished."

There had been only minor changes in Massachusetts probation since its establishment in 1878. The system had a deeply rooted provincial cast; it was decentralized, with virtually all policy and practice decisions, except those governed by statute, made at the local level. The central office was poorly staffed and without real authority. Standards of practice did not exist. To borrow from political scientist Michael Lipsky (1980), probation in 1975 was a pure form of "street level bureaucracy."

The organizational atmosphere at that time can best be captured by identifying three characteristics of the system: (1) probation as rehabilitation, (2) decentralization, and (3) probation by personality.

1. Probation as Rehabilitation

Massachusetts probation during the 1970s was driven primarily by the "social work/medical model" that had been predominant in probation throughout most of the 20th century. In this model, the probation officer (PO) was seen primarily as an advocate/counselor for the probationers. The obligation to enforce court-ordered conditions was acknowledged, but aspects of control, monitoring, surveillance, and individual deterrence were clearly of secondary or tertiary importance, and subordinated to helping the client.

2. Decentralization

The organizational structure in 1975 approached total decentralization. Some 100 probation offices were organized by county for payroll and budgetary purposes, but there was no specific accountability beyond the local office. The central office had no clearly established system for oversight of each office, and hence, by default, local autonomy was the order of the day.

3. Probation by Personality

Each office had its own established routines and de facto standards. Instead of being codified either locally or centrally for the sake of uniformity, departmental practices and procedures varied considerably around the state and usually reflected the personality of the chief probation officer.

The probation landscape is vastly different ten years later. The watershed year was 1978. The Massachusetts court reorganization act of that year provided, among other provisions, for the consolidation of the many individual offices into one state system (previously POs were county employees) under an enhanced and revitalized central authority. The legislation specifically required that the commissioner of probation develop, promulgate, and monitor standards of practice in all major areas of probation practice. The commissioner was both empowered and directed to exercise "executive control and supervision" over probation personnel throughout the state.

In 1979, an experiment began with a uniform case classification system. Parenthetically, it was potential PO/departmental liability that was a driving force behind this classification proposal. The purpose of the trial period was to test the feasibility of a single method of offender assessment and supervision plan development. This would evolve in 1980 into the institutionalization of a risk/need classification system statewide—a system that remains in place, with some modification, to the present. Starting in 1980, a series of statewide standards began to be promulgated. The staff of the central office grew throughout this period and, in time, regional administrators were designated to oversee compliance with standards and to offer technical assistance to probation offices in their regions. During this period, standards were developed for supervision, investigation, management information system, office procedures, risk/need and probation standards.

THE PRESENT: ASSESSING THE CURRENT SITUATION

A second component of the sociopolitical environment concerns "those present situations and events that are of such significance that they will influence decision making" (Twain, 1983: 33). By 1985, Massachusetts probation had three "focal concerns"—(1) risk control, (2) centralization, and (3) probation by standards—which reflects a reconceptualization of the structure and purpose of probation.

1. Risk Control/Community Protection

Supplanting offender-oriented rehabilitation as the aim of probation today is the (socially oriented) goal of community protection through risk control.

This philosophical shift has been reflected in a variety of policy changes, including the use of a risk prediction scale, an increasing emphasis on holding offenders accountable through high rates of probation surrenders, the introduction of surveillance-like probation conditions (curfews, employment and residence verification, etc.), plus a de-emphasis on direct provision of rehabilitative service and, instead, a reliance on employing a network of referrals in the community. In other words, the idea of probation officers as "therapists" is strongly discouraged.

2. Centralization

In 1978 the various county probation systems were consolidated into one state system. With the support of the chief administrative justice of the trial court, the then commissioner of probation moved assertively into a role of authority by designating regional probation administrators (RPAs) to represent the commissioner in each of seven geographic regions. For the first time, a clear and operational chain of command from the local office to a central state authority was established.

3. Probation by Standards

The nearly complete discretion in probation practice that existed in 1975 was greatly diminished by 1985. Standards had been promulgated in all major areas of the probation officers' work. Extensive training in the standards and technical assistance to aid implementation took place. By 1985, most standards had undergone three or four major formal monitorings with written feedback to the commissioner and to the local office manager (chief probation officer).

Particularly in the initial stages of standards implementation, there was a good deal of resistance to centrally imposed guidelines. Many probation officers clearly preferred a wide range of choice in handling their caseloads. It was suggested that "creativity" had been stifled in the service of greater accountability. Yet, increased accountability has made those doing good work more visible, but it also has identified those whose work is inadequate—a development which has caused some added tension.

By late 1985, the degree of resistance to uniform standards had greatly subsided. While there are still pockets of resistance, there is a general effort to conform to standards. This is in part due to the dissipation of resistance over time (as it becomes clear that standards are permanent, though modifiable), and in part due to the infusion over the last seven years of new personnel who much more readily accept the existing system. Nonetheless, it should be noted that at least part of the resistance to "new" reforms, such as intensive probation supervision, is a carryover from the continuing resistance to "old" reforms, such as objective risk assessment.

Specifics of the Experiment

Prior to 1985, when the IPS experiment began, Massachusetts probation officers worked with a case classification system that had been continually refined and revalidated. Since its inception, two university-based research projects have validated the accuracy of the risk instrument utilized in the system.

The strength of this system allowed the agency to address experimentally a growing and obvious need in the Massachusetts system—that is, the need for an intensive probation supervision system for certain high risk offenders. State legislative initiatives (including the recent presumptive sentencing bill), nationwide developments in progressive probation practice, and the need to be part of the solution to a growing correctional crisis all pointed to the need for developing such a program.

Generally, those offenders assigned to such a program would receive the following specialized supervision:

1. Increased levels of personal and collateral contacts;

2. Increased emphasis on mandatory referrals to meet social and/or personal needs related to criminal behavior;

3. Strict enforcement of probation conditions.

The IPS program is premised on the assumption that certain high risk/high need offenders can be handled more effectively through an enhanced community supervision strategy. This strategy would center around strict enforcement of conditions of probation emphasizing the following:

• Careful and thorough assessment of offender risk and need.

• Concerted effort toward surveillance and control of the offender's activities for greater public safety.

• Addressing the offender's needs that are contributing to illegal behavior. The rule of thumb is that the POs should restrict themselves to needs that are strongly and consistently related to the reduction of criminal behavior.

• Identification and involvement of appropriate community resources which, through referrals, can contribute to the reduction of criminal behavior.

The dual emphasis—strict client accountability and the addressing of identified needs—increases the likelihood of dealing effectively with the highest risk offenders currently under probation supervision. By establishing a constant presence in the life of the probationer who has presented both a past threat to the community and a high level of individual need, probation could prove to be a cost-effective response to the problem of public safety. A comparison of the differences between the highest level of supervision in the existing system and the new higher level intensive supervision requirements appears in Table 1.

PRINCIPLES FOR MANAGING CHANGE

1. *Principle:* Make Change a Policy

Changes that come within an agency as spasms are unlikely to succeed. A body at rest will tend to stay at rest. Kurt Lewin's (1951) model of "freezing-unfreezing and re-freezing" is unhelpful or misleading in this respect. An organization that is expected to remain tightened against change, or is told that change will only occur when it is crucial, will have the most difficulty adapting to change efforts. A refrozen organization, however recently unfrozen, is well defended against the next round of changes. Kanter (1983) has suggested a different way of thinking about those organizations that will adapt to change most successfully. She

Table 1

A Comparison of Maximum Supervision
Under Existing System With
Intensive Supervision Experimental System

	Maximum Supervision	*Intensive Supervision*
1. Selection Criteria:	Probationers with initial risk/needs scores of 10 or less (in a matched sample of non-participating courts)	All probationers with initial risk/needs scores of 10 or less (15 pilot courts)
2. Minimum Contacts:	Two (2) contacts per month	Ten (10) contacts per month, four (4) direct and six (6) collateral
3. Initial Client Assessment:	Based on one contact and subsequent case review (routine procedure for all new cases)	Full investigation during first 30 days on probation; requirements include multiple personal and collateral contacts (in addition to regular contacts)
4. Referral Procedures:	All referrals are at discretion of probation officer (except mandatory referrals by judges)	Mandated referrals in all high need areas identified in classification (in addition to any mandated referrals by judge at sentencing)
5. Record Checks:	Not required	Required every 30 days through Probation Central File (PCF)
6. Revocation Policy:	Local, discretionary	Mandatory case review and strict four-stage revocation policy
7. Supervision Style:	Traditional, based on a generalized investigation of problems/needs	Brokerage emphasizing investigation and follow-up referrals in three specific need areas: substance abuse, employment and counselling

describes the healthy organization as always operating "on the edge of its competence," looking constantly for ways to innovate and improve performance. The image is one of a fluid, responsive organization, constantly unfrozen.

Practice: Nearly one year prior to the announcement of the IPS program, a newly appointed agency head announced that while he had not decided on any new policies, members of the organization could expect fairly constant change during his tenure. He spoke of the constantly changing legal/political/social environment in which probation operated and hence the need for an adaptive, proactive organization. As his reputation in the organization rested on his recent engineering of changes in case classification and management information systems, this announcement of "change as policy" was given credence. Therefore, his announcement of the IPS program some ten months later caught no one by surprise.

2. *Principle:* Forecast for Change

In addition to making change a policy, the specific nature of any planned change can and should be anticipated. Many organizations fail to anticipate, forecast, or imagine the future so that change can be planned for and anticipated. This makes for a reactive organization that, while willing and committed to change, is behind the curve as to specifics. While forecasting changes in an organization's external environment is a tricky and imprecise business at best, attending to some key environmental factors is crucial and can prevent being "blind-sided." An organization's leaders must envision the agency's future at least three to five years ahead. Social psychologist Karl Weick (1979) of Cornell refers to this as the need for an organization to see its environment and to develop sensors for important external cues. Similarly, Kanter (1983) refers to the necessity for organizational "blueprints and forecasts" even if they are later departed from in practice.

Practice: In addition to announcing a commitment to change, the agency head made it his principal responsibility to constantly interact with legislative and executive branch leaders, members of the local academic community, citizens and public service groups, the business community, key members of the judiciary—anyone who was likely to have a hand in shaping the immediate future of the state criminal justice system. In doing so, it became clear almost immediately that many key people foresaw the probation agency as the major factor in solving a growing prison overcrowding problem. While nothing official had been said or written, it was clear that both a sentencing alternative commission and relevant legislation was going to receive serious attention. This "forecasting" allowed the agency to get moving on its own experiment before anyone had a chance to impose policy or programs from outside. Ultimately, this meant that the agency was able to design that part of later legislation that called for the use of IPS.

3. *Principle:* Develop a Strategy for Change

Many innovations have failed because the change process or strategy had not been consciously thought out or developed. David Twain (1983: 96) puts it succinctly: "Establishing program objectives without giving much thought to how they will be attained will almost certainly lead to difficulties." Clear and Gallagher (1985: 436), in discussing examples of successful and unsuccessful case classification systems in probation, offer the following: "Failure to approach classification as a complicated planned change has been the primary reason why so many agencies fail to implement effective systems."

As much thought must be given to how something is to be implemented as to the intrinsic nature of the change itself. This leads to the question of a recommended model for change. The typology of change strategies developed by Chin and Benne (1976) refers to change being either "Empirical Rational" (i.e., those to be changed are moved to change on the basis of the logic of its necessity), "Normative Re-Educative" (i.e., the attitudes and values of those to be changed are developed in line with the needed change), or "Power Coercive" (i.e., those to be changed do so for fear of the consequences if they do not). However, treating these strategies as discrete types implies the choice of one over the other, which oversimplifies the problem and restrains effectiveness in planned change.

An alternative perspective envisions the combination of many diverse approaches to producing change. The philosopher Mortimer Adler (1983) has written on the nature of persuasive speech, borrowing from the ancient Greek rhetoricians in suggesting that any attempt to persuade others must address "Logos" (the reason for change), "Ethos" (what is to be valued in the change), and "Pathos" (why those to be changed should be emotionally committed to change). John Kenneth Galbraith (1983), in *The Anatomy of Power,* discusses the use of "condign" (coercive), "compensatory" (that which is based on a reward or fair exchange), and "conditioned" power (that power which works through positive, benign, influence and an identification with the personality or values of the change agent).

Practice: In the implementation of the IPS program, as much thought was given to how to effect the change as was given to the components of the program itself. First, it was felt that it would be essential for the agency head to personally sell the program to each of the experimental courts ("Ethos," "conditioned power") on an individual as well as broup basis. Following implementation, the agency head remained involved on a nearly daily basis in the answering questions from the field and monitoring the initial IPS case assessments, copies of which, as with other probation cases, are sent from the field to the central office.

In a day-long group meeting with the experimental courts, held two months prior to the program inception, the agency head shared with the managers the rationale ("Logos") for the program in light of likely future developments in the state. It was explained that this experiment would allow the agency to essentially dictate the nature of the programs mandated in future legislation ("compensatory"), whereas simply waiting for legislative proposals would leave the agency in a reactive, "eleventh hour" position. Since it was an experimental program, without new funding or sanction (yet) by the legislature, it was impossible during the experiment to offer any tangible rewards to the experimental courts. Instead, both in the initial meetings, subsequent training, and interim progress report meetings, the agency was careful to involve the entire staff. In addition, the agency's quarterly journal consistently contained references to the project. In summary, a variety of change strategies were being used simultaneously with hope that the combined effect would be sufficient.

4. *Principle:* **Accept Resistance as Normal**

Donald Klein (1976) discusses the bias against those who resist change and the corresponding inclination to see resisters as pathologically opposed to anything new. Klein emphasizes that this bias will alienate those to be changed and prevent the possibility of cooperation and collaboration in the change effort. Opposition to change, says Klein, is healthy and, indeed, useful. Established practice has developed over time to allow the job to be done in a way that all participants in the system can accept. Established practice is inextricable from the self-esteem, competence, and autonomy of the worker and, therefore, any attack on it will be felt as an attack on these values. For change to be effective, Klein writes, a respectful hearing must be given to the legitimate concerns of experienced and knowledgeable members of the work force, and accommodations made whenever possible. Those leading the change, if they wish it to succeed, must open up a dialogue with staff both in recognition of their personal investment in "things-the-way-they-are" as well as to avail themselves of advice on shortcomings in the proposed change.

Once again, some of the literature most illuminating of this principle is a step or two removed from the mainstream organizational develop-

ment literature. Paulo Friere (1970: 122), a Brazilian educator of international reputation, said this about change in an analogous context:

> Dialogue with the people is radically necessary to every authentic revolu-
> tion. This is what makes it a revolution, as distinguished from a military
> coup. One does not expect dialogue from a coup—only deceit (in order
> to achieve "legitimacy") or force (in order to repress). Sooner or later,
> a true revolution must initiate a courageous dialogue with the people.
> Its very legitimacy lies in that dialogue. It cannot fear the people, their
> expression, their effective participation in power. It must be accountable
> to them, must speak frankly to them of its achievements, its mistakes,
> its miscalculations, and its difficulties.

Practice: The resistance to implementation of IPS followed "normal"
and predictable lines. In a previous work (1986), the authors delineated
some of the specific types of resistance manifested in the early stages of
the project. A variety of resistance strategies were employed by POs who
fear loss, failure, or the unknown. These strategies include: (1) *ritualism*
(i.e., doing the paperwork, but not following the risk/needs assessment);
(2) *denial of ownership* (i.e., rather than carve out a control-oriented role
for supervision, the PO denies ownership in the program; e.g., "it's the
Commissioner's idea, not mine, so don't blame me"); and (3) *rebellion* (i.e.,
failure to fill out the risk/need forms correctly for marginal IPS cases).

In the early stages of the project, these negative manifestations were
common, but they dissipated over time. As a method for defusing
resistance, the views and reactions of managers were continually
monitored. From the first discussion of the planned changes with field
staff, their input was invited and several large and well attended forums
were created to allow them an opportunity to provide their opinion of
the program. While it was explained that, given the present and likely
future realities impinging on probation, the program needed to be implemented, their views as to any major flaws in design were invited and,
whenever possible, accommodated. Quite deliberately, there was a good
deal of flexibility built into the administration of the program so that local
managers who wished to experiment with a specialist or team approach
(in lieu of a generalist approach) could do so.

In addition, once the program was established all participants were encouraged to notify the central office of any problems or questions. In the
initial four months of implementation, these calls were taken directly by
the agency head, so as to signal the importance attached to field personnel's concerns and reactions to the programs.

For example, the original model called for maintaining the offender at
an intensive level of supervision for the duration of the project. Many
field personnel told the central office that an adjustment downward at

the ten-month level, irrespective of the risk score and predicated on success and cooperation to that point, would both provide an incentive to the offender who had been placed on probation for two or more years and would save time, an important consideration to the local office managers.

In addition, the managers had a great deal of concern about the data collection process (e.g., how much time was involved, how intrusive would the process be to the local office, how much support staff assistance was expected). At one of several statewide meetings held with the managers involved in the experiment, the research team discussed their proposed procedures but made several significant changes based on input from the managers. In general, the research team agreed to do as much of the "grunt" work (e.g., pulling and refiling folders) as was necessary. This offer to take away as much of the burden of data collection as possible from the managers made them more agreeable to what was clearly a disruptive process.

5. *Principle:* Conduct Change as an Experiment

Daniel Patrick Moynihan (1969), in his studies of the programmatic failure in the federal "War on Poverty," emphasized the limits of social science knowledge and hence the need to institute policy reform in the social services as tentatively as possible. Broad-based, comprehensive and permanent change is almost certain to fail, according to Moynihan, unless opportunities are provided for close monitoring and mid-course (or earlier) corrections when experience suggests they are necessary. "Social science habitually overcompromises," according to Moynihan, and a certain humility and circumspection among policy workers is prudent and crucial.

Quinn (1980) refers to the usefulness of a policy of "logical incrementalism" as an antidote to overreaching in change efforts. This theory suggests that any agency undertaking change would do well to try a little change in a few places and see what happens. A period for refining and debugging proposed change before it becomes fully implemented increases the likelihood of eventual success and prevents having to fight continual rear-guard actions—as happens when the change is presented as a fait accompli.

Practice: Because the IPS program was conceived and implemented well in advance of a legislative mandate, there was ample time to experiment and design an optimal program. As it turned out, by the time the legislature did come calling, the agency was able to preempt any legislative design by recommending that the pilot program be taken as a guide to legislative action. In addition, a number of problems were resolved through program modifications that would be built into the final proposal for a statewide program. The pilot courts had understood that their feedback was essential and would affect the final product. And the experimental nature of the program made some practical difficulty with it easier to accept.

SUMMARY

The five principles enunciated above reflect an interweaving of theory and practice in managing change in probation. In cross-fertilizing theoretical approaches with actual experience, both are enhanced— theories are refined, and empirical testing and practice benefit from some useful academic constraints. In doing so, the criminal justice academic and the criminal justice practitioner, for a time, travel on convergent tracks and their worlds become desegregated.

CODA

As this paper is being written, the experimental program is 15 months into implementation. As compared with the difficulties experienced with the initial implementation of a case classification system six years earlier, the process of change this time has been much smoother and without significant strain or controversy, as measured by documented levels of compliance and complaints channeled through the regional administrators.

REFERENCES

Adler, Mortimer (1983). *How to Speak, How to Listen.* New York: MacMillan.

Bennis, Warren G., Kenneth D. Benne, Robert Chin and Kenneth Corey (1976). *The Planning of Change.* New York: Holt, Rinehart and Winston.

Chin, Robert and Kenneth D. Benne (1976). "General Strategies for Effecting Change in Human Systems." In *The Planning of Change,* edited by Warren G. Bennis and others. New York: Holt, Rinehart and Winston.

Clear, T.R. and K.W. Gallagher (1985). "Probation and Parole Supervision: A Review of Current Classification Practices." *Crime & Delinquency* 31(3): 423-443.

Cochran, Donald, Ronald Corbett and James M. Byrne (1986). "Intensive Probation Supervision in Massachusetts: A Case Study in Change." *Federal Probation* L(2): 32-41.

Friere, Paulo (1970). *Pedagogy of the Oppressed.* New York: Seabury Press.

Galbraith, John Kenneth (1983). *The Anatomy of Power.* Boston: Houghton Mifflin.

Kanter, R.M. (1983). *The Change Masters.* New York: Simon & Schuster.

Klein, Donald (1976). "Some Notes on the Dynamics of Resistance to Change: The Defender Role." In *The Planning of Change,* edited by Warren G. Bennis and others. New York: Holt, Rinehart and Winston.

Lewin, K. (1951). *Field Theory in Social Science.* New York: Harper and Row.

Lipsky, Michael (1980). *Street-level Bureaucracy: Dilemmas of the Individual in Public Services.* New York: Russell Sage.

Moynihan, Daniel Patrick (1969). *Maximum Feasible Misunderstanding.* New York: Free Press.

Quinn, J.B. (1980). *Strategies for Change: Logical Incrementalism.* Homewood, IL: Richard D. Irwin.

Twain, David (1983). *Creating Change in Social Settings.* New York: Praeger.

Weick, K. (1979). *The Social Psychology of Organizing.* Reading, MA: Addison-Wesley.

Intensive Supervision: Officer Perspectives

by
John T. Whitehead
Charles A. Lindquist

Much of the current research on intensive supervision is either descriptive (program details) or evaluative (recidivism and cost-benefit data). This chapter examines the perspectives of line officers working in an intensive supervision program in a southern state. Both participant observation and survey questionnaires were used to examine officer perceptions of the program, job satisfaction, job stress and burnout. The findings indicated that officers reacted favorably to the program and to extensive interaction with offenders; however, several problem areas, such as officer work shortcuts and lack of resources for assisting offenders with concrete adjustment problems, were discerned. Comparisons with regular parole officers, and some suggestions for program improvement, are offered for consideration.

Despite the serious problem of expanding prison populations, control of offenders in the community is currently under scrutiny for both policy and pragmatic reasons. From the standpoint of policy, the mission of community supervision is under intense debate; some continue to emphasize offender needs (Dietrich, 1979), others call for an emphasis on offender surveillance (Conrad, 1982), and some call for new conceptualizations that integrate past models or go beyond past models to focus on justice (Fogel, McAnany and Thomson, 1980), public safety (Fogel, 1984), or risk control (Clear and O'Leary, 1983; O'Leary and Clear, 1984). Pragmatically, reexamination of community sanctions is occurring because of increased concern about the amount of crime committed by offenders under supervision in the community, and because recent research has indicated that a considerable amount of crime is committed by felons sentenced to probation (Petersilia, Turner, Kahan and Peterson, 1985).

One partial solution to both the policy and the pragmatic problems of community sanctions is a new type of intensive supervision offering a clearer focus on surveillance and specifically seeking to prevent recidivism. This type of intensive supervision incorporates strict curfews, work or community service requirements, and frequent checks of selected offenders in order to create an intermediate level of punishment. Unlike the intensive supervision programs of 15 years ago, which often incorporated reduced caseloads without any concomitant changes in supervision practices (Carter and Wilkins, 1976: 394), the most recent forms of intensive supervision are perceived to stress offender accountability (Bennett, 1986). Judges, police, and the public have been promised, explicitly or implicitly, that the offenders in such programs will be watched and watched closely.

The rationale and objectives of the current intensive supervision programs are quite clear. What is not so evident is how line officers are reacting to the programs and how they are implementing the goals which policymakers have set for intensive supervision. As McCleary (1978) demonstrated in his study of a traditional parole agency, supervision in practice is often quite different from supervision in theory; the needs, values, perceptions, and attitudes of the line officers shape parole. This suggests that any complete examination of intensive supervision must include data on the officers who implement the program, since such street level bureaucrats (Lipsky, 1980) ultimately determine the fate of any innovation.

Such an examination of intensive supervision workers is particularly necessary in view of findings that traditional parole officers avoid contact with parolees or, at best, either seek contacts that are "typically, amiable, superficial, and brief" (Stanley, 1976: 97), or regard at least some offenders as troublesome if they make more than minimal demands on officer time (Norland and Mann, 1984). While such superficial supervision has been attributed to high caseloads (Stanley, 1976) and thus should not be a problem in intensive supervision, other possible reasons for the problem cannot be ignored. These include parolees' desires to avoid officer surveillance (Irwin, 1970), officer laziness and involvement in personal pursuits (McCleary, 1978), and the lack of a fully developed service technology, i.e., the resources to provide practical assistance to parolees (Studt, 1973). If superficial supervision is indeed occurring, then it is hard to envision how the new intensive programs will be any more effective than the older ones, which, at best, produced mixed results and/or did no worse than institutional programs in terms of offender recidivism (Lundman, 1984; Sechrest, White and Brown, 1979).

In addition to being critical to policy implementation, the attitudes and perceptions of the officers are worthy of study in their own right. While concern for the occupational problems of community supervision workers is not new (see Ohlin, Piven and Pappenfort, 1956; Studt, 1973), it is only recently that researchers have devoted more detailed attention to the job satisfaction of probation and parole employees (Polisky, 1981a, b), job stress and job burnout (Whitehead, 1985; 1986a, b; Whitehead and Lindquist, 1985). Research on worker attitudes and perceptions is important in clarifying the problems officers may be experiencing so that appropriate interventions can be initiated. This is particularly important among officers in intensive supervision because these workers have been ignored in prior research.

To address these issues—both the impact of line personnel on the new intensive supervision programs, and the effects of the programs on the attitudes and perceptions of the line officers— we conducted participant observation and administered questionnaires to all of the officers in the Alabama Supervised Intensive Restitution (SIR) Program in its first year of operation (1984), and then conducted a follow-up study the next year. For purposes of comparison, we also administered the same survey instrument to all of the probation and parole officers in the state involved in traditional supervision.

SIR originated as what Blumstein (1983) has called a "back-door" prison population-reduction strategy. Faced with court pressure to alleviate prison overcrowding and intolerable conditions, the Alabama Department of Corrections reclassified a number of state inmates so that they became eligible for community supervision. The inmates were then transferred to the community, where they were placed under intensive supervision by correctional officers. While SIR was initially based on existing restitution statutes and laws permitting confinement to be extended to the community, this "relief-valve" program was formally legitimized by the legislature in late 1983. At present writing (June 1986), about 750 selected state inmates are under intensive community supervision by correctional officers.

The intensive supervision officers studied were unique because they were correctional officers working in a program developed and operated by the Alabama Department of Corrections. Most other intensive supervision programs are probation or parole agency programs employing probation/parole officers. In other respects the Alabama program is very much like any other intensive program: it involves small caseloads (presently about 30 offenders per officer) of selected offenders who must be employed or perform community service, pay a supervision fee, pay restitution when ordered, observe a curfew, and abide by rules quite similar to those in intensive probation/parole programs. Inmates selected for intensive community supervision are mainly property offenders within three years of a parole review date (or expiration of sentence) who have acceptable institutional records and suitable sponsors.

The program officers, who do not retain any institutional responsibilities, act essentially as parole officers; they enforce the conditions of the program and also attempt to assist the "inmates" with their adjustment problems. Thus, the experiences and attitudes of the Alabama officers, though technically correctional officers, are relevant for all line personnel working or about to work in intensive supervision.

FINDINGS: PARTICIPANT OBSERVATION STAGE

In December 1983, we conducted participant observation research by accompanying six of the 35 intensive supervision officers as they interacted with offenders. This research strategy was designed to obtain a qualitative and phenomenological sense of intensive supervision and of officer perceptions, prior to the survey stage of our research. Despite the brevity of our participant observation, several interesting findings were noted.

First, the intensive supervision officers reported great satisfaction with their jobs. They mentioned the challenge, the variety ("something different every day"), and being out of the prison setting. One officer also noted that SIR is a high priority program within the department of corrections; he was told that it is "a privilege" to be assigned to the program. He also felt that promotional opportunities might be greater for SIR employees than for institutional guards. Another officer indicated he would not accept a promotion if it meant he would have to leave the program for assignment to a major institution.

Second, as McCleary (1978) observed in regular parole, intensive supervision is open to officer shortcuts to increase free time. One of the officers we observed noted that he resorted to telephone curfew checks of offenders even though the rules stipulated in-person checks. The officer was aware the "inmate could go out right after the call, but he could do that right after a visit too." Thus, the officer rationalized his shortcut by claiming it was no less effective than a face-to-face contact. In a similar vein, another officer visited a gas station to check on an offender who was supposed to be working as a mechanic. Although the offender was not present, the officer accepted the employer's explanation that the individual would be coming to work later. After securing a pledge from the employer that he would call the officer if the mechanic did not show up for work, the officer left, commenting that involving the employer was a good way to handle this type of situation. By diffusing the responsibility for supervision, the officer seemed satisfied with this type of contact.

Third, as Studt (1973) pointed out in her study of California parole, community supervision often lacks a technology of service. During a visit by a team of two officers conducting a curfew check, it was observed that one offender was living in a house where the heat had been turned off due to nonpayment of the utility bills. The offender asked for permission to work in Georgia, claiming he had a friend there who might have a job for him, but the officers noted that even the governor could not authorize the offender's out-of-state employment. The officers advised the man to turn to them for help if he had any other problems, but they had no assistance for his lack of heat. Similarly, these same officers had nothing but sympathy to offer to a woman inmate who had received a denial from the nursing board to have her nursing license reinstated. Nevertheless, we did observe some successful service provision. Some officers provided employment leads and explained how offenders could go about obtaining drivers' licenses. In addition, one officer prided himself on his appearance in court with several offenders who were delinquent in child support payments, so that he could explain the program to the local judge in order to "buy time" for the offenders to make up their payments. Nevertheless, while officers frequently talked about the counseling or advice they were providing to offenders, our observation indicated that practical assistance was often beyond their capabilities.

Fourth, as might be expected, the officers possessed considerable discretionary power, including the power to recommend the immediate transfer of an offender from the program to an institution. (As the program progressed, officers even acquired the power to decide if they would accept back on their caseloads an offender previously transferred from the program to prison.) Officers used their discretion to bend the rules for particular inmates. During an evening curfew check, for example, it was observed that a relatively young female offender was living by herself. Since offenders were required to live with their respective sponsors, the officers were asked why she was living alone. The officers indicated that she was having trouble with her mother, who wanted her to be "nice" to several older men; hence, the officers permitted her to live away from her sponsor-mother. Offenders and their respective sponsors seemed to be aware of the officers' discretionary power; as a result, some offenders and sponsors made requests to the officers and indicated that they wanted to personally help the officers. For example, one officer was checking on an offender who was working in her father's junkyard. The officer happened to mention that he might be interested in purchasing an engine from a wrecked car as a replacement for the engine in his personal car. The sponsor-father indicated he not only would be happy to sell the engine at a quite reasonable price, but would arrange for a friend to install the engine, also at a reasonable price. As in any type of intensive supervision program, then, officers were faced with considerable temptations.

Another problem was equipment. The department of corrections car used by one team had over 100,000 miles on the odometer and seemed to be burning transmission fluid. Lack of radio communication in the event of an emergency concerned the officers, as did a lack of air conditioning in one of the state vans. Finally, the fact that there was only one car available for the two-officer team prevented each of them from going out alone and thus being more efficient.

A final problem observed was that the intensive supervision officers believed departmental policy against carrying a weapon was unwise. One officer said, "A man would be a fool not to protect himself," so he carried a gun. Interestingly, the officers still felt safer on the streets than in prison, where "you never know if you're coming out." One officer noted, for example, that in prison an officer does not always know the names of all the inmates he comes in contact with, or else an inmate may think the officer will not be able to identify him. Thus, an inmate may feel freer to attack a prison guard than a SIR client would feel about attacking a SIR officer.

FINDINGS: SURVEY RESEARCH STAGE

While our participant observation was limited, it did provide some clues about officer reactions to intensive supervision. Accordingly, we decided to structure a survey instrument designed to tap officer perceptions of job satisfaction and job stress. Recognizing that job stress can become pronounced among workers who have intensive contact with clients, and that such stress can produce "a syndrome of emotional exhaustion and cynicism" (Maslach and Jackson, 1981: 99), we also decided to focus on the phenomenon of job burnout.

Overall job satisfaction was measured by the item included in *The 1977 Quality of Employment Survey* (Quinn and Staines, 1979): "All in all, how satisfied would you say you are with your job?" To measure the sources of job satisfaction, respondents were asked to describe, in open-ended fashion, the three most satisfying aspects of their jobs. Level of job stress was measured by the item developed by Smith and Ward (1983) in their study of southeastern police officers: "How stressful do you consider your job to be?" To measure the sources of job stress, respondents were asked an open-ended question about the three most stressful aspects of their job. Job burnout was measured by the 22-item Human Services Survey developed by Maslach and Jackson. (Formerly entitled the Maslach Burnout Inventory, the 1981 survey was used by permission of Consulting Psychologists Press.)

The three subscales of the Human Services Survey—emotional exhaustion, depersonalization, and lack of personal accomplishment—relate to aspects of the burnout syndrome. Emotional exhaustion is measured by nine items, such as "I feel burned out from my work." Depersonalization is measured by five items concerning callous or impersonal treatment of offenders, while lack of personal accomplishment is measured by eight items that concern such matters as the degree of the worker's positive influence on the lives of clients. All of the burnout items are measured on seven-point frequency and intensity scales. Because the frequency measures correlate highly with the intensity measures, only the former are reported. Reliability coefficients for the subscales were as follows: emotional exhaustion, .86; depersonalization, .70; and lack of personal accomplishment, .70.

Because only 35 officers were assigned to the SIR program at the time of our research, a maximum response rate was required; hence, all 35 were given questionnaires at a training session in May 1984. Administration in this fashion produced a 100 percent response rate. Since our personal observations had indicated that the SIR officers were acting essentially as parole officers, questionnaires also were mailed to all 125 line probation/parole officers in the state, thereby providing a basis for comparison. Eighty-six percent (N = 108) of the probation/parole officers responded. The magnitude of the probation/parole officer response rate indicated a strong likelihood that respondents were representative of this population.

There were significant differences between the two groups. Twenty-five percent of the intensive supervision officers were black, 49 percent were college graduates, and the average length of correctional employment was five years. Only 7 percent of the probation/parole officers were black, 92 percent were college graduates, and the average length of correctional employment was 15 years. Intensive supervision officers had an average caseload of 35 offenders; they reported spending an average of 24 hours per week in direct contact with offenders and 15 hours per week on paperwork. Probation/parole officers, who had an average caseload of 122, reported spending an average of only 13 hours per week in direct client contact but 24 hours per week on paperwork.

Job Satisfaction

The intensive supervision officers reported a significantly higher level of overall job satisfaction than the probation/parole officers. For example, 63 percent of the intensive supervision officers were "very satisfied" with their jobs, and none were "not too" or "not at all satisfied." Only 44 percent of the probation/parole officers were "very satisfied" and 11 percent were "not too" or "not at all satisfied."

As indicated by Table 1, the responses of both groups to the open-ended questions regarding the sources of job satisfaction were analyzed for common themes. Content analysis indicated that most sources of satisfaction could be subsumed under one of the following four categories: (1) positive aspects of client contact (e.g., helping offenders cope with problems and changing offender outlooks), (2) autonomy and variety (e.g., flexibility and encountering different situations), (3) extrinsic factors related to employment (e.g., salary and job security), and (4) administrative factors (e.g.,

Table 1

Job Satisfiers and Job Stressors by Worker Category

Job Satisfiers	Worker Category	
	SIR Officers	*Probation/Parole Officers*
Positive Aspects of Client Contact	77%	66%
Autonomy/Variety	54%	40%
Extrinsic Factors	11%	30%
Administrative Factors	6%	16%
Job Stressors		
Negative Aspects of Client Contact	43%	42%
Overload	37%	63%
Extrinsic Factors	43%	7%
Administrative Practices	14%	20%
	(N = 35)	*(N = 108)*

Note: Percentages do not add up to 100% because officers could list more than one satisfier and stressor.

working as a team member and having good co-workers). While the rank order of job satisfiers was the same for both groups, more of the intensive supervision officers reported greater satisfaction from the positive aspects of client.contact and from experiencing autonomy and variety in their jobs than did the probation/parole officers. More of the latter reported greater satisfaction from extrinsic and administrative factors than did the intensive supervision officers.

Perhaps the most surprising finding was that three-quarters of the intensive supervision officers reported contact with offenders to be one of the most satisfying aspects of their jobs. Further examination of the responses of the intensive supervision officers who reported satisfaction from offender contact indicated four related types of satisfaction. First, a number of the SIR officers simply enjoyed helping offenders. Typical of such responses were the remarks of a rural SIR officer who derived satisfaction from "listening to problems that an inmate encounters during his adjustment period and assisting the inmate to readjust to community life with his family and job assignment." Similar comments indicated that the intensive supervision officers perceived a major component of their role to be providing assistance to the offender; for these officers intensive supervision was not merely surveillance. Second, a number of the SIR officers obtained satisfaction from seeing an inmate successfully complete the program and be granted parole. Third, several officers enjoyed interaction with the families and sponsors of inmates. Fourth, quite a few officers simply seemed to enjoy interacting with inmates on a one-to-one basis.

Over half of the intensive supervision of officers mentioned autonomy and/or variety as a positive feature of their jobs. One respondent noted that an officer could "work the hours you want to and work the job the way you see fit"; another officer enjoyed "making decisions" and encountering "something different just about every day"; still another enjoyed working "almost totally unsupervised." Such positive experiences contrast markedly with the lack of autonomy perceived by prison guards (Lombardo, 1981; Cheek and Miller, 1983) and the boredom of institutional routine (Lombardo, 1981).

Only a small percentage of the intensive supervision officers made specific positive comments about administrative factors or extrinsic matters such as pay and benefits. An interesting secondary finding was that several officers reported satisfaction because their jobs allowed them to associate and work with other "law enforcement personnel"; accordingly, we infer that SIR officers perceived themselves as law enforcement officers, even though so many mentioned offender assistance as the most satisfying aspect of the job. As has been found elsewhere (Toch and Klofas,

1982; Cheek and Miller, 1983), it appears that officers often do not perceive a conflict between the law enforcement and assistance aspects of their role. Parenthetically, we noted during our participant observation that some officers bent over backwards to provide services for their law enforcement colleagues. One officer frequently transported state-sentenced prisoners from several county jails within his geographic area to the prison system's main classification center and then returned with recently released SIR inmates to deliver them to their respective sponsors. This practice helped him gain acceptance from the county sheriffs, and the officer found that deputy sheriffs would pass on information from their sources about the behavior of offenders on the officer's caseload.

Job Stress

The intensive supervision officers reported a significantly lower level of job stress than the probation/parole officers. For example, 23 percent of the SIR officers felt that their job was "very" or "more than moderately" stressful, and 46 percent felt that their job was "slightly" or "more than slightly" stressful. On the other hand, 49 percent of the probation/parole officers reported their job to be "very" or "more than moderately" stressful, and only 14 percent reported slight or more than slight stress.

As also indicated by Table 1, the responses of both sets of workers to the open-ended question regarding the sources of job stress were again analyzed for common themes. Content analysis indicated that most sources of stress fit under one of the following four categories: (1) negative aspects of client contact (e.g., having to make arrests and not being able to solve an offender's problems), (2) overload (e.g., inadequate time to complete assignments), (3) extrinsic factors (e.g., lack of equipment and office space), and (4) administrative practices (e.g., supervisory inconsistency and lack of effective communication). The rank order of job stressors was somewhat different for each group of workers. While roughly the same percentage of intensive supervision officers reported negative aspects of client contact, overload, and extrinsic factors as stressors, distinctions were more pronounced among the probation/parole officers. More of the latter reported overload stressors, followed by negative aspects of client contact and administrative practices.

It is interesting to note that client contact appears to be a double-edged sword for both intensive supervision officers and probation/parole officers. Positive client contact provides the greatest source of job satisfaction for both groups, yet negative client contact is the greatest source of job stress for intensive supervision officers and the second greatest source of stress for probation/parole officers. Further examination of the responses of the intensive supervision officers who reported stress from offender contact indicated three related types of stress. First, a number of SIR officers reported stress stemming from client characteristics. Several officers reported stress from "dealing with uneducated, lower economic class people," and the tendency of some offenders to lie to officers (e.g., "going to an inmate's house after you have talked to him/her on the telephone and they are gone or hiding"). In addition, some officers were concerned about the potential for violent behavior by their clients. Second, many of the intensive supervision officers appeared to be frustrated in their attempts to help offenders. Such frustration was generated when officers either interacted with inmates who were perceived as not trying to rehabilitate themselves, or when officers saw motivated offenders experiencing a lack of support from their respective environments (e.g., "rejection on the community's part toward an inmate"). Third, several of the intensive supervision officers reported stress stemming from the perception that they were responsible for the behavior of their clients. For example, a female officer said she was "afraid I will be [held] responsible if an inmate messes up."

Thirty-seven percent of the intensive supervision officers reported problems with overload, such as being required to supervise offenders dispersed over a wide geographic area, and working long hours away from home. As noted above, several officers felt that they were "on call" all the time. Others reported some difficulty with "completing all the paperwork on time and getting it in."

Low pay, equipment problems, and night curfew checks represent most of the extrinsic factors mentioned by 43 percent of the officers. The night curfew checks were problematic because they were "unusual" (compared to a 9-to-5 job) and because of the possible danger associated with them. For example, while we accompanied two officers during a late evening curfew check in a low income, public housing project, one officer commented: "Would you come in here by yourself? Don't you think that we should be paid the same as [higher paid] parole officers?" Thus, officers were concerned about the safety of making late night contacts even though, as one officer noted, such curfew checks were considered "most important—must be continued for success [of the program]."

Only a relatively small percentage of the intensive supervision officers made negative comments about administrative practices. Those who did referred to such problems as "lack of communication from administration to the field officer" and "written policies occasionally unclear."

Job Burnout

When the mean burnout scale scores for the two groups of workers were compared, the only significant difference was in emotional exhaustion. Intensive supervision officers reported feeling this aspect of burnout less frequently ($\overline{x} = 1.56$) than the probation/parole officers ($\overline{x} = 2.24$). In the SIR group, the negative aspects of intensive offender supervision were problematic for only a few individuals. The overwhelming majority were not experiencing the feelings of emotional exhaustion that both leading burnout theorists (Maslach, 1982; Cherniss, 1980) posit as stemming from intensive contact with clients.

FINDINGS: FOLLOW-UP STAGE

Because the findings reported above indicated such positive perceptions on the part of the intensive supervision officers, especially when compared to the perceptions of probation/parole officers, we became concerned that a Hawthorne effect might be present. This led us to re-administer the same questionnaire, one year later, to all remaining members (N = 27) of the 1984 cohort of SIR officers. (Among the other eight officers, five had either transferred or were reassigned to institutions, and three were no longer employed in corrections.)

There was no significant decline in overall job satisfaction; over half of the intensive supervision officers reported that they were "very satisfied" with their jobs and, again, none were "not too" or "not at all" satisfied. Although this measure indicated more or less the same level of job satisfaction, we did note some changes in reported sources of satisfaction. Positive aspects of client contact were reported as a job satisfier by 48 percent of the officers (down from 77 percent in 1984). The percentage reporting autonomy/variety as a job satisfier remained about the same, while slightly more than one-third reported extrinsic and administrative factors as satisfiers (up from about 10 percent in 1984). The typical officer, then, reported a decrease in satisfaction from the positive aspects of client contact and an increase in satisfaction from extrinsic and administrative factors. Officers appeared to report somewhat less satisfaction from helping offenders, considerably less satisfaction from interaction with the families and sponsors of inmates, and about the same amount of satisfaction from seeing an inmate complete the program and from personal interaction with offenders. Characteristic of these changes were the responses of a rural officer who initially reported satisfaction from "helping inmates adjust to free world living," "supervising one's self," and "understanding [the] judicial system." One year later, the same officer reported satisfaction from "freedom from 8-5 grind" and the "people I work with."

There was no significant increase in the level of job stress; in fact, reported stress declined slightly. Only 15 percent of the intensive supervision officers felt their jobs were "very" or "more than moderately" stressful, and 37 percent felt their jobs were "slightly" or "more than slightly" stressful. While this measure showed more or less the same level of job stress, we did see some changes in reported sources of stress. Negative aspects of client contact were reported as a job stressor by 77 percent of the officers (up from 43 percent in 1984), while percentages reporting stress from the other three sources remained more or less the same. Typical of this change were the responses of an urban officer who initially reported stress from "[being] unfamiliar with certain aspects of the job" and "not receiving full support from the home office." One year later, the same officer reported stress from "inmates constantly calling at home all hours night and day," and "forcing inmates to meet curfew and report for community service."

Looking at the three related types of stress from offender contact discussed earlier, several observations can be made. Stress stemming from client characteristics—especially concern about the potential for violent behavior on the part of their clients—appeared to increase, as did the frustration of seeing clients receive inadequate support from their families and/or sponsors. Finally, the stress arising from the perception that officers were responsible for the behavior of their clients also increased.

In summary, then, the double-edged sword which client contact represents may have undergone some changes. Qualitatively, the positive edge appears to be slightly duller, while the negative edge seems to cut somewhat more deeply. However, our quantitative findings of no significant differences over time regarding levels of job satisfaction and job stress force us to remember that client contact is only one aspect of these two phenomena. In a similar vein, paired t-tests showed no significant differences over time regarding mean scores on any of the three burnout subscales. Based on the complete set of findings, then, we have found no convincing evidence of a Hawthorne effect. Generally speaking, intensive supervision officers perceive their jobs as satisfying and only slightly stressful. Furthermore, the stress of intensive client contact has not been of sufficient magnitude to lead to job burnout.

DISCUSSION

The first summary conclusion is that the SIR officers were overwhelmingly positive about their job experiences in intensive supervision. Based on our observation of officers and on our quantitative (see Lindquist and Whitehead, 1986a, b) and qualitative analyses of the survey questionnaires, the vast majority of officers were satisfied with their jobs and preferred intensive supervision to work in a prison setting. We think that such positive reaction is not simply a sense of relief from all the problems associated with the institutional work setting but is also a positive reaction to the job of intensive supervision. That is, we think that the SIR program's more precise definition of mission, which provides greater officer role clarity, is largely responsible for the positive attitudes of the officers. The program has avoided much of the role conflict and ambiguity present in previous community supervision efforts (Studt, 1973), and has thereby forestalled some of the most important sources of job dissatisfaction, stress, and burnout (see Cherniss, 1980, for a discussion of the causes of job burnout). Thus, we hypothesize that probation or parole officers transferred from regular supervision to intensive supervision programs with a similar mission and clarified officer role would be as positive in their job attitudes and perceptions as the SIR officers.

The second major finding is the positive reaction of the SIR officers to increased offender contact; the officers derived satisfaction from perceiving themselves to be of assistance to inmates released to community supervision. Thus, our findings provide partial confirmation for Lombardo's hypothesis that correctional officers "as well as inmates reap the benefits when correctional officers meet the challenges of helping inmates cope with stress" (Lombardo, 1982: 296). Similarly, our findings add to the list of empirical studies showing that "the correctional orientation of officers includes not only advocacy of punishment but also healthy support of rehabilitation . . ." (Cullen, Link, Wolfe and Frank, 1985: 513).

Moreover, the finding that intensive supervision correctional officers enjoy working with law enforcement officials indicates that the officers themselves do not automatically feel any role conflict between assistance and control (a finding supported by Cheek and Miller, 1983: 116; Toch and Klofas, 1982: 43). Again, we hypothesize that this would also be the case with probation/parole officers working in intensive supervision. Research on probation/parole officer job burnout has found that such officers consistently respond favorably to statements such as "I deal very effectively with the problems of my probationers/parolees," and "I feel exhilarated after working closely with my probationers/parolees" (Whitehead, 1984, 1985). Moreover, contrary to Maslach's theory (1982), client contact was not a source of job burnout for probation officers; contact bore no statistically significant relationship to emotional exhaustion or depersonalization, and was associated with more frequent feelings of personal accomplishment (Whitehead, forthcoming). Thus, it is our conclusion that officers in intensive supervision programs react positively to a clearly defined emphasis on surveillance that does not exclude the service aspects of the job.

All is not well in intensive supervision, however. There is some indication that officers may cut corners to create free time just as parole officers have done in the past (McCleary, 1978). Given the unrealistic demands placed on SIR officers, this is not unexpected. Our observations and our survey research indicated that officers may be required to begin work at 7 a.m. to get some offenders started at community service tasks or make employment checks, and then be expected to make curfew checks late that same evening. Perhaps a solution is to formally authorize some of the officer shortcuts; for example, a number of telephone checks of offenders could be allowed to reduce the unrealistic demands on line officers. Such telephone contacts are a formal part of the intensive supervision program in New Jersey (Pearson, 1986). Similarly, many officers reported feeling on call 24 hours a day, seven days a week. That officers were so positive about their jobs despite such demands is probably a reflection of both the mission and role clarity of the SIR program and a sense of relief at being released from the prison setting with all of its negative factors. Both the SIR program and similar programs will have to deal with this issue of unrealistic demands on line personnel. Research on probation/parole officers, for example, has found that quantitative overload (not having enough time to get everything done) is an important correlate of job burnout (Whitehead, 1984, and forthcoming).

The finding that officers at times did not have the resources to assist offenders with concrete problems is not new. Years ago, Studt (1973) found this very same problem in parole. Her solution was for the parole department to devote more attention and financial aid to improving the technology of service, and not merely developing proficiency in the technology of surveillance. Specifically, she recommended economic support during reentry, status clearance services, emergency service, support for parolee employment, restoration of civil rights, and other measures as components of an adequate service technology. Perhaps the biggest problem in enhancing the service capabilities of officers is political; intensive supervision programs are being sold and justified to the public as less expensive alternatives to incarceration. As Irwin (1980) has pointed out, community correctional programs with adequate service provision are not inexpensive.

A final note is a call for continued research on the perceptions and opinions of the officers who conduct the supervision in the new intensive programs. Our findings on the positive attitudes of the SIR officers indicate that line officers can be very committed to the success of such intensive supervision programs and that they have insightful suggestions on how to enhance the programs. To ignore the role that line employees play in the implementation of such alternatives to incarceration is to risk the danger that the actual programs will never achieve the results so many policymakers expect from intensive supervision.

REFERENCES

Bennett, L.A. (1986). "A Reassessment of Intensive Service Probation." Paper presented at the 1986 Annual Meeting of the Academy of Criminal Justice Sciences in Orlando, FL.

Blumstein, A. (1983). "Prisons: Population, Capacity and Alternatives." In *Crime and Public Policy*, edited by J.Q. Wilson. San Francisco: Institute for Contemporary Studies.

Carter, R.M. and L.T. Wilkins (1976). "Caseloads: Some Conceptual Models." In *Probation, Parole, and Community Corrections* (2nd ed.), edited by R.M. Carter and L.T. Wilkins. New York: John Wiley & Sons.

Cheek, F.E. and M.D. Miller (1983). "The Experience of Stress for Correction Officers: A Double-bind Theory of Correctional Stress." *Journal of Criminal Justice* 11: 105-120.

Cherniss, C. (1980). *Staff Burnout: Job Stress in the Human Services.* Beverly Hills, CA: Sage.

Clear, T.R. and V. O'Leary (1983). *Controlling the Offender in the Community.* Lexington, MA: Lexington.

Conrad, J.P. (1982). "Can Corrections be Rehabilitated." *Federal Probation* 46(2): 3-8.

Cullen, F.T., B.G. Link, N.T. Wolfe and J. Frank (1985). "The Social Dimensions of Correctional Officer Stress." *Justice Quarterly* 2: 505-528.

Dietrich, S.G. (1979). "The Probation Officer as Therapist." *Federal Probation* 43(2): 14-19.

Fogel, D. (1984). "The Emergence of Probation as a Profession in the Service of Public Safety: The Next Ten Years." In *Probation and Justice: Reconsideration of Mission,* edited by P.D. McAnany, D. Thomson, and D. Fogel. Cambridge, MA: Oelgeschlager, Gunn and Hain.

——P.D. McAnany, and D. Thomson (1980). "Probation as the Pursuit of Justice." Paper presented at the International Seminar on Community Corrections at Niagara Falls, NY.

Irwin, J. (1970). *The Felon.* Englewood Cliffs, NJ: Prentice-Hall.

——(1980). *Prisons in Turmoil.* Boston: Little, Brown.

Lindquist, C.A. and J.T. Whitehead (1986a). "Correctional Officers as

Parole Officers: An Examination of a Community Supervision Sanction." *Criminal Justice and Behavior* 13: 197-222.

——and J.T. Whitehead (1986b). "Guards Released From Prison: A Natural Experiment in Job Enlargement." *Journal of Criminal Justice* 14: 283-294.

Lipsky, Michael (1980). *Street-level Bureaucracy: Dilemmas of the Individual in Public Services.* New York: Russell Sage.

Lombardo, L.X. (1981). *Guards Imprisoned: Correctional Officers at Work.* New York: Elsevier.

——(1982). "Alleviating Inmate Stress: Contributions From Correctional Officers." In *The Pains of Imprisonment,* edited by R. Johnson and H. Toch. Beverly Hills, CA: Sage.

Lundman, R.J. (1984). *Prevention and Control of Juvenile Delinquency.* New York: Oxford.

Maslach, C. (1982). *Burnout: The Cost of Caring.* Englewood Cliffs, NJ: Prentice-Hall.

—— and S.E. Jackson (1981). "The Measurement of Experienced Burnout." *Journal of Occupational Behaviour* 2:99-113.

McCleary, R. (1978). *Dangerous Men: The Sociology of Parole.* Beverly Hills, CA: Sage.

Norland, S. and P.J. Mann (1984). "Being Troublesome: Women on Probation." *Criminal Justice and Behavior* 11:115-135.

Ohlin, L.E., H. Piven, and D.M. Pappenfort (1956). "Major Dilemmas of the Social Worker in Probation and Parole." *National Probation and Parole Officer Journal* 2: 211-225.

O'Leary, V. and T.R. Clear (1984). *Directions for Community Corrections in the 1990s.* Washington, DC: U.S. Department of Justice.

Pearson, F.S. (1986). "Taking Quality Into Account: Assessing the Benefits and Costs of New Jersey's Intensive Supervision Program." Paper presented at the Annual Meeting of the Academy of Criminal Justice Sciences in Orlando, FL.

Petersilia, J., S. Turner, J. Kahan and J. Peterson (1985). "Executive Summary of Rand's Study, Granting Felons Probation: Public Risks and Alternatives." *Crime & Delinquency* 31: 379-392.

Polisky, R.J. (1981a). "Enhancing the Job Satisfaction of Probation and Parole Officers. Part I." *Corrections Today* 43(1):78-85.

——(1981b). "Enhancing the Job Satisfaction of Probation and Parole Officers. Part II." *Corrections Today* 43 (2): 54-95.

Quinn, R.P. and G.L. Staines (1979). *The 1977 Quality of Employment Survey.* Ann Arbor, MI: Survey Research Center, University of Michigan.

Sechrest, L., S.O. White and E.D. Brown, eds. (1979). *The Rehabilitation of Criminal Offenders: Problems and Prospects.* Washington, DC: National

Academy of Sciences.

Smith, B. and R. Ward (1983). "Stress on Military and Civilian Police Personnel." *American Journal of Police* 3:111-126.

Stanley, D.T. (1976). *Prisoners Among Us: The Problem of Parole.* Washington, DC: Brookings Institute.

Studt, E. (1973). *Surveillance and Service in Parole: A Report of the Parole Action Study.* Washington, DC: U.S. National Institute of Corrections.

Toch, H. and J. Klofas (1982). "Alienation and Desire for Job Enrichment Among Correction Officers." *Federal Probation* 46(1): 35-44.

Whitehead, J.T. (1984). "Probation Mission Reform: Implications for the Forgotten Actor—the Probation Officer." *Criminal Justice Review* 9 (1): 15-21.

———(1985). "Job Burnout in Probation and Parole: Its Extent and Intervention Implications." *Criminal Justice and Behavior* 12:91-110.

———(1986a). "Job Burnout and Job Satisfaction Among Probation Managers." *Journal of Criminal Justice* 14:25-35.

———(1986b). "Gender Differences in Probation: A Case of No Differences." *Justice Quarterly* 3:51-65.

———(forthcoming). "Probation Officer Job Burnout: A Test of Two Theories." *Journal of Criminal Justice.*

———and C.A. Lindquist (1985). "Job Stress and Burnout Among Probation/Parole Officers: Perceptions and Causal Factors." *International Journal of Offender Therapy and Comparative Criminology* 29:109-119.

Taking Quality Into Account: Assessing the Benefits and Costs of New Jersey's Intensive Supervision Program*

by
Frank S. Pearson

Benefit/cost analyses of correctional programs are often sketchy, invalid, or both. Using standard cost-effectiveness analysis is often an inadequate solution; hidden errors lurk in that approach as well. The external evaluation research on New Jersey's Intensive Supervision Program is confronted with the problem of assessing some hard to quantify, but real benefits of the program. Specific problems in benefit/cost analysis, and how the researchers are dealing with the problems, are discussed.

* Paper presented at the Academy of Criminal Justice Sciences annual meeting, March 20, 1986. Research funding has been provided by the U.S. National Institute of Justice, Grant Number 83-IJ-CX-K027. I have benefited from comments on this topic made by Gail S. Funke and by Jackson Toby, who is a co-principal investigator on the project.

BACKGROUND OF THE RESEARCH PROJECT

Although New Jersey's Intensive Supervision Program (ISP) is a complex program with many facets, it reflects four paramount goals:

a. to release selected offenders from incarceration into the community after they serve three or four months of their prison terms in order to make scarce prison space available for more serious offenders.

b. to provide alternative, appropriate, intermediate punishment in the community for those selected offenders instead of prison sentences.

c. to control deviant behavior by those selected offenders while they are in the community.

d. to run the program at costs significantly lower than the costs of incarceration.

There are seven major program components of New Jersey's ISP intended to function collectively as *means* to the four ISP goals. In developing these program components, ISP administrators looked at, and learned from, intensive supervision programs in Georgia, New York and Texas. The essential structure of the New Jersey ISP can be grasped most easily by a brief description of each component.

Intensive Supervision Contacts

The program was designed to handle a total active caseload of 375 to 500 offenders.

Participants are contacted by their officers at least 20 times per month during the first 14 months of the 18 month program. Of the 20 contacts, during the first six months in the program at least 12 are face-to-face, usually in the participant's home, occasionally at work. The remainder of the 20 contacts per month are by telephone. Also, at least four of the 20 contacts are curfew checks late at night to make sure that the participant is obeying the curfew: the general rule is that each ISP participant must be home every night from 10 p.m. to 6 a.m.

After successfully completing the first six months that might be termed the beginners' phase in the program, the intensity of supervision is gradually lessened through subsequent intervals as intermediate participants, then advanced participants and finally senior participants.

Employment or Vocational Training

The program rules state that failure to be employed or in an educational or vocational training program, without good cause, after the first 90 day period will result in a return to prison. The participant must present all pay stubs to the ISP officer as verification of employment, and the officer requires similar documentation of satisfactory progress in educational programs. The program has been remarkably successful in maintaining high levels of employment, considering the backgrounds of the offenders and normal turnover (e.g., due to seasonal work): the unemployment rate has been around 5 percent.

Community Service Work

The program requires at least 16 hours of community service by each participant per month. By design, most of the community service work is physical labor (such as sweeping and mopping), and this contributes to the goal of providing a level of punishment that is intermediate between probation and imprisonment.

Community Sponsor and Network Team Support

Each participant is to have a community sponsor and other support persons who monitor the participant's progress and provide help and guidance. For example, the program participant's community sponsor sees him or her regularly, offers encouragement and points out problems that may arise. In addition to contacting the offender, the ISP officer also talks to the community sponsor as another way of monitoring the offender's progress in the program. An example of a network team member's support is providing transportation to and from work for the offender.

Special Counseling

Many participants take part in weekend evening group counseling scheduled by their ISP officer. Most participants also take part in one or more specialized counseling programs for drug abuse, alcohol abuse, gambling, family problems, minor emotional or psychological problems, and financial problems.

Individual Responsibility

A great deal of emphasis is placed on the participant's taking responsibility for his actions and for straightening out his life. This is one of the points that the resentencing panel of judges emphasizes as it reviews each participant's progress at the end of the person's beginner, intermediate, advanced, and senior stages in the program.

Selective Intake of Offenders

The selection of participants is a careful and complicated process involving seven separate steps or "levels of eligibility."

Any applicant whose current conviction is for homicide, robbery, or a sex crime, or whose sentence includes a minimum term of incarceration that must be served, is not eligible to participate in the Intensive Supervision Program. Of the crime types eligible for further consideration, most are burglaries and major thefts, small time drug sales, and fraud.

Our involvement with New Jersey's Intensive Supervision Program for controlling felons in the community is that of independent researchers. We have had access to all ISP files, talked to ISP officers and participants in the field, have collected comparison data from the department of corrections and the state police, and have interviewed scores of policymakers in New Jersey's criminal justice system.

REVENUE AND EXPENDITURE STATEMENTS AS INDICATORS OF THE BENEFITS AND THE COSTS OF A CORRECTIONAL PROGRAM

Naturally, many program assessments focus on revenue and expenditure statements as indicators of the benefits and costs. For example, a report on a five year examination of the Incarceration Diversion Unit in Lucas County, Ohio included this section:

> The cost savings of this program were determined from the commitment rate reduction brought about by the program. Each offender diverted by the program led to an incarceration cost savings of $6,788 per year of incarceration time. Assuming an average time served of 17 months for the Ohio reformatory system, this results in a savings of $9,617 per offender diverted. Obviously, these were not all the costs and benefits which accrue to the program. Incarcerated offenders do not pay taxes (income lost by the state), and their families frequently draw welfare benefits. On the other hand, they do not draw unemployment, should they otherwise be eligible. There were a host of these costs and benefits which could be used to calculate these analyses, however, the assumption was that these second-level costs and benefits would 'zero out' and that the major consideration was direct cost to the state (Latessa, 1984:5).

Another example is the 1984 report on Georgia's intensive supervision program (Erwin, 1984: 60-61). The Georgia evaluation lists itemized costs for the Intensive Probation Supervision program, including costs of office space, travel, and equipment. The total program costs per year were about $900,000— approximately $1,600 per IPS probationer.

Since the available evidence suggested that the probationers in the program would have been incarcerated if the program did not exist, comparisons were made with incarcerated offenders. Total prison costs in

Georgia per offender per year were about $11,000. Obviously, $1,600 for an IPS participant compares favorably with $11,000 per incarcerated offender.

On the benefit side, the earnings and payments produced by the IPS group in one year were itemized, adding the aggregate earnings (including taxes paid, restitution, fines, and probation fees) and the estimated value of community service work performed. The total came to roughly $1.5 million. The report stated that "[i]f these offenders had been incarcerated this income production would have been impossible and we must assume that families would necessarily have sought support from other sources including welfare assistance" (Erwin, 1984: 66).

To compare the benefits versus costs of the IPS, the Georgia evaluation does two things. First, the total revenue figure per year of about $1.5 million seems to have been compared with the total expenditure figure of about $900,000. This appears to be the basis for a statement that "it is clear that the benefits exceed the cost of the program" (Erwin, 1984: 67). The second component of the overall comparison involves the principle that the return on the programmatic investment should exceed the return available from the realistic alternatives. This is the concept of *opportunity costs* (Mishan, 1982: 64; Rossi and Freeman, 1982: 274-275; Wayson, Funke and Falkin, 1984: 26). Because prison was the realistic alternative, the cost difference of only $1,600 per offender-year for IPS versus $11,000 per offender-year for prison is cited again to support the conclusion that IPS has a higher return on investment. In addition, the evaluation report notes that although crime in general may not have been significantly reduced by the program, no IPS probationer had been convicted of any crime of violence (Erwin, 1984: 67).

Estimates also have been made of the costs and benefits of New Jersey's Intensive Supervision Program. The first estimate of costs to gain wide circulation was made early in 1983, before the program began operations. The estimate was that ISP could be expected to cost about $5,000 per offender per year. The average annual cost to maintain an inmate in a New Jersey prison at that time was about $15,000 (New Jersey Administrative Office of the Courts, 1983: 2-3).

State of New Jersey budget figures for July 1, 1984 through June 30, 1985 showed that ISP cost approximately $1.6 million for the year. The average active caseload from July 1984 through June 1985 was about 235 offenders. That comes to roughly $7,000 per offender-year, while prison costs were roughly $17,000 per offender-year. By December 1985 the active caseload had reached 350, while the total program cost was about $1.5 million.

If we follow Georgia's approach and total the earnings and payments produced by an ISP active caseload of 235 at that time—including the aggregate earnings, taxes paid, restitution, fines, probation fees, and estimated value of community service work performed—the total comes to roughly $2.5 million. Using this approach, New Jersey too can infer that the benefits exceed the cost of the program.

Because prison was in fact the alternative for these people, the cost of $7,000 per offender-year for ISP versus roughly $17,000 per offender-year for prison can be cited as a rough indication that ISP has a higher return on investment than imprisonment would for these offenders.

SOME EVALUATION STATEMENT OPTIONS

It is not wrong to present the estimates on benefits and costs in the way that was done for Ohio and for Georgia as long as the limitations are understood, but there are alternative approaches that ought to be considered. Some of the paired options discussed below are not mutually exclusive, and they can both be used in the research.

One Perspective or Multiple Perspectives

One set of options a researcher can consider is to present one perspective or multiple perspectives in the analysis. It is common for benefit/cost assessments to present figures from a single, undefined perspective. This can lead to some strange benefit-bedfellows. For example, in the Georgia report aggregate earnings (including taxes paid and assessments collected) and the estimated value of community service work were added together to estimate total benefits. The weakness of that approach is that the earnings benefit the probationer, but the probationer probably views the taxes, restitution, fees, and community service as costs. On the other hand, law abiding citizens may consider tax revenue and the fees collected as benefits, but the probationers' income is not clearly beneficial to citizens in general. This is the issue of the real *distribution* of benefits and costs (Weiss, 1972: 86; Rossi and Freeman, 1982: 287).

Some experts in benefit/cost analysis recommend an alternative approach of listing benefits and costs by more homogeneous groups. For example, Wayson, Funke and Falkin (1984:47-48) recommend such separate categories as society, the criminal justice system, and the individual.

Unrealistic Assumptions or Problematic Measurements

In doing research on complex programs in the criminal justice system, precise information often cannot be obtained. Nevertheless, we have to provide the best information we can about those areas, imperfect though it may be. The options include (a) basing the analysis on some *assumptions* that are probably unrealistic, or (b) not making such strong assumptions, but rather relying on problematic, rough *measurements*. Do we rely on an assumption that will allow us to proceed with a straightforward analysis knowing that the assumption is likely to be false, and hope that the assumption is not so erroneous as to make the conclusions completely invalid? Or, do we limit our assumptions to those that are realistic, and proceed with the analysis by developing rough estimates of factors that cannot be measured accurately? For example, in the Ohio report the *assumption* was made that such benefits and costs as tax revenues, welfare benefits, and unemployment compensation would offset one another. The magnitude of those benefits would be roughly equal to the magnitude of those costs. Another approach is trying to present rough estimates of those specific benefits and costs, problematic though the measurements may be. For some purposes, rough measurements are better than none at all. When the assumptions would be very shaky and measurements would have to be very rough estimates, it would be better to use both approaches. If the resulting analyses agree with each other, one can have some confidence in the benefit/cost conclusions.

Net Benefit and Benefit/Cost Ratios or Qualitative Evaluation

A third general set of options is to report a net benefit figure and perhaps a benefit/cost ratio, or presenting qualitative assessments. Quantitative estimates are very valuable in their appropriate domains. The Ohio report concentrates on quantitative estimates. The Georgia report mentions the human benefits of having an offender remain in his home with his family and the social costs of new crimes, but a choice was made to focus on well accepted quantitative variables such as revenues and costs. It would be better to include *all* important consequences that clearly stem from a program, including the unscaled, qualititative consequences. Why not include as lines on the summary page factors that do not have a definite monetary value? Examples of such summary page items might include "the humane value of averting 350 person-years of incarceration each year (e.g., 350 offenders each serving one year less)" and, to give another example, "the value of 6 new felonies probably averted per 350 offenders per year" (if the program group averaged 6 fewer felonies per year than those occurring in a reasonable comparision group, controlling for extraneous factors). In general, it might be preferable to include a final summary page in most benefit/cost analyses that would include benefit/cost ratios and net benefit figures, and *also* describe unscaled qualitative consequences as well; then, decision makers can weigh those qualitative variables as they think appropriate (cf. Research and Education Association, 1982:71).

"All-or-nothing" or Multi-level Options

A fourth set of options is to assess benefits and costs on an all-or-nothing basis or, instead, to consider multiple levels. The all-or-nothing approach is easier: it contrasts the presence of the budgeted program with the complete absence of the program. Another option, albeit more difficult, is to consider not only the presence or absence of the currently budgeted program but also other optional levels of budgeting. For example, a four-level analysis might consider the consequences of having (1) no such program at all, (2) the program at current total caseload levels, (3) the same program with a somewhat smaller caseload, and (4) the program with somewhat larger caseload. This approach provides at least a rough idea of the *marginal* net benefit of the program (see, for example, Thompson, 1980:92; Mishan, 1982:16). Decision makers may well ask, "If it is demonstrated that the ISP program is of net benefit, would it be relatively more cost-beneficial on a larger scale (or, for that matter, on a smaller scale)?"

ATTEMPTING TO EXPAND THE STATEMENT BASE: TENTATIVE PLANS FOR THE NEW JERSEY PROJECT

Additional Perspectives

Table 1 is consistent with Wayson, Funke and Falkin's suggestion of categorizing the benefits and costs of a program by affected groups; in this instance, New Jersey citizens, ISP participants and, for some items, other specific groups.

Adding Some Problematic Measurements

Use of criminal justice system resources. Our measure of the use of scarce prison space *may* be problematic, but rough estimates are better than no estimates at all, as long as their limitations are understood. First, assuming a fixed stock of prison space (and associated facilities) per year, selectively giving the less serious offenders less time in prison than was previously the case (on the average) necessarily leaves more space per year for the more serious offenders.

This logical assessment will be supplemented with empirical estimates of shifts in the use of prison space. The ISP group will be examined in

Table 1

Plans for Categorizing the Benefits and Costs of New Jersey's Intensive Supervision Program (ISP): Some Examples.

Benefits and Costs:

	1. Use of CJS Resources
for N.J. citizens (in general)	Quantitative assessment of consequent use of prison space. Cost-effectiveness compared to ordinary-term-of incarceration (OTI) sample.
for ISP participants	Chosen by them.
	2. General Monetary Consequences
for N.J. citizens	Tax revenues collected during time ISP participants would have been in prison; fees paid to ISP.
for ISP participants	Net earnings during the time ISP participants would have been incarcerated.
for others: crime victims	Differences in restitution and in payments to a general victim compensation fund, compared to OTI.
children	Child support payments during the time ISP participants would have been incarcerated.
	3. New Crimes Committed
for N.J. citizens	Re-arrests and re-conviction rates compared to OTI.
for ISP participants	Rates of subsequent incarcerations compared to OTI.
	4. Impact on Just Desserts
for N.J. citizens	Satisfaction of just desserts.
for ISP participants	Choice rate compared to OTI.
	5. Other Non-monetary Consequences
for N.J. citizens	Public opinion on ISP vs. prison.
for ISP participants	Impact on drug/alcohol abuse. General orientation to life.
for specific community groups	Estimated value of community service at minimum wage rate.

relation to comparable offenders. A computer program for random sampling was used to select 500 offenders sentenced to prison between January 1, 1981 and December 31, 1981, excluding cases that would not have been eligible for ISP (for example, all crimes of violence were excluded from the sampling). Those dates allowed time for all of these third and fourth degree felons to be released from prison under parole in the community during a period close to that when the ISP group was in the community.

From this ordinary-term-of-imprisonment (OTI) comparison group we can calculate how long those similar types of offenders actually served in prison compared to the prison time of the ISP group, and estimate the number of offender-days in prison ISP has saved. The quantity of offender-days saved frees space for first and second degree offenders.

Also, comparative cost estimates can be made that could be useful to New Jersey citizens. We know what prisons the ISP offenders were in and the annual per capita cost of those prisons. (Because they are predominantly minimum security facilities, the typical cost per offender-year may actually be a couple of thousand dollars lower than the $17,000 cited as a preliminary rough estimate.) We also know that the ISP group averaged about four months in the prisons before being released to ISP, and we can determine how long our comparison group stayed in prison before release on parole.

General monetary consequences. In addition to the standard revenue and cost items that have been mentioned (for example, taxes and fees collected), it seems sensible to list some measurements that can only be given very problematic monetary values, but which are important quantitative variables nevertheless. Unemployment rates are one example. At the time of sentencing for their offense, about 30 percent of ISP participants were unemployed. At this point in our study we can at least say that during their stay in the program fewer than 10 percent are unemployed in any given month. (Typically, the unemployment rate has been around 5 percent.) Of course, the earnings made during the time the ISP participants would have been incarcerated will be compared to a baseline for the ordinary term of imprisonment group.

We shall also value community service at the minimum wage rate. On the one hand, we know that some professional and skilled work was provided as community service; this work would be undervalued at minimum wage rates. On the other hand, some of the community groups might not have been willing to pay even minimum wage rates for other tasks, but agreed to the community service for altruistic reasons, to help the participant and the Intensive Supervision Program; that part of the community service would be overvalued, even using the minimum wage estimate.

However, using the minimum wage rate is a conventional compromise estimate. Those who disagree with this approach could redo the analysis using a higher or lower estimate of the worth of the community service.

New crimes committed. Our indicators of the program impact on the rate and seriousness of new crimes will include the number of arrests for felony offenses per intervals of time "at risk" in the community; for example, for a standard risk interval of one year, the rate of ISP participant felony arrests. Another useful indication of this program outcome will be estimates of the average time to a felony arrest for that subset who have had a felony arrest. The same analyses will be performed for felony convictions, misdemeanor arrests and misdemeanor convictions. For all of these variables we will have comparison data from our ordinary-term-of-imprisonment group.

Including Qualitative Evaluation

Quantitative measurements—even when expanded to include rough, problematic measurements—are unlikely to cover all of the important benefits and costs of an intensive supervision program. In addition to presenting those numerical estimates, we would like to list the following for decision makers and other interested parties to consider and to weigh in the balance as they see fit.

Impact on "just deserts." The criminal justice system is not viewed by everyone as utilitarian. Many citizens believe that criminal justice is based, at least in part, on a concept of just deserts; that is, particular crimes are viewed as intrinsically meriting a certain degree of punishment. Therefore, the consequences of ISP in terms of just deserts should be mentioned. The program was planned to be an intermediate level of punishment between ordinary probation and longer periods of imprisonment. There is no one true valuation on this issue, of course. Some citizens apparently think that ISP establishes a better balance of just deserts. Others may view early release from prison as being unjustly lenient. Still others think that for any nonviolent offenders (not just those in ISP) imprisonment is excessively severe.

These are real values implicated in policy decisions, and they deserve consideration.

Other non-monetary consequences. It is also appropriate to include a *qualitative* assessment of the impact of ISP on prison space. This would include judgments of the seriousness of the problem of exceeding designed capacity and the value of freeing a certain amount of prison time and space. Also, from the point of view of the offenders, the overwhelming majority show by their actual choices that they prefer intensive supervision to continued imprisonment.

Another non-monetary consequence is linked with the fact that 70 percent of the offenders admitted into ISP have a serious health problem; namely, drug abuse or alcohol abuse. We can measure changes in substance abuse while in the program because urine samples are taken randomly and tested for the presence of drugs (including marijuana and alcohol). Declines in drug use and alcohol use (if the participant is diagnosed as having an alcohol problem) are qualitative consequences worth discussing.

There are other qualitative assessments worth noting in a benefit/cost analysis, if we acknowledge that they are not very *objective* measurements. For those in special counseling programs, these might include the percent rated (by those conducting the sessions) as "improved." There also are miscellaneous indications of personal responsibility on the part of participants; for example, parents reporting that the participant is now fulfilling his responsibilities around the house, a spouse reporting that child support payments have been made in full and on time, etc. (for other examples, see Wayson, Funke and Falkin, 1984:103,120). It is even worthwhile to mention comments made by former ISP participants when they are no longer under ISP control. This would include comments about ISP made by graduates and also from those who were ejected from the program and returned to prison. For example, after graduating from New Jersey's ISP one man wrote to the program director expressing his appreciation, including the following remarks:

> In all honesty, this program gave me a chance to prove myself as a law abiding citizen, and to be quite frank with you, I am very pleased with myself today. [My ISP officer] should be very highly commended on the job he does for the program. Not only does he act as an authoritive [sic] figure, but most importantly, he is a friend. I feel that it is important for an officer to have a close relationship with the state prisoners. Communication is the key to success in this program as I see it.

Multi-level Options: Rough Estimates of Marginal Costs

If possible, in addition to the standard approach of comparing the consequences of having the ISP program at the current level of about 300 active participants versus having no ISP program at all, we would like to obtain at least rough estimates of the benefits and costs likely to be associated with caseloads of 200, 400 and 500 offenders. These could be used to get at least a rough idea of the *marginal* net benefit of the program. It seems reasonable to assume economies of scale and that the program would be more cost-effective with 400 or 500 participants, but can we actually estimate how much more economical it is likely to be?

CONCLUSION

Benefit/cost analyses of correctional programs are often sketchy, invalid, or both. Using standard cost-effectiveness analysis is often an inadequate solution, because often important variables are not brought into focus. The external evaluation research on New Jersey's Intensive Supervision Program is confronted with the problem of assessing some hard-to-quantify—but real—benefits of the program. The way we are planning to approach the difficulties is by expanding the focus of the benefit/cost analysis. The expanded analysis includes specifying particular affected groups, reporting admittedly problematic measurements of important outcome variables, reporting purely qualitative assessments of some non-quantifiable variables, and trying to examine multi-level program options and estimate marginal net benefits.

REFERENCES

Erwin, Billie S. (1984). *Evaluation of Intensive Probation Supervision in Georgia.* Atlanta, GA: Georgia Department of Offender Rehabilitation (August).

Latessa, Edward J. (1984). "The Incarceration Diversion Unit: A Five Year Examination." Paper presented at the annual meeting of the American Society of Criminology at Cincinnati, OH.

Mishan, E.J. (1982). *Cost-Benefit Analysis.* London: George Allen and Unwin.

New Jersey Administrative Office of the Courts (1983). Intensive Supervision Program. Trenton, NJ.

Research and Education Association (1982). *Handbook of Economic Analysis.* New York: Research and Education Association.

Rossi, Peter H. and Howard Freeman (1982). *Evaluation: A Systematic Approach.* Beverly Hills, CA: Sage.

Thompson, Mark S. (1980). *Benefit-Cost Analysis for Program Evaluation.* Beverly Hills, CA: Sage.

Wayson, Billy L., Gail S. Funke and Gregory P. Falkin (1984). *Managing Correctional Resources.* Washington, DC: U.S. National Institute of Justice.

Weiss, Carol H. (1972). *Evaluations Research,* Englewood Cliffs, NJ: Prentice Hall.

The Effectiveness of Intensive Supervision with High Risk Probationers*

by
Edward J. Latessa

This study examines the effectiveness of providing intensive supervision to a group of high risk felony probationers over a one year period. In order to determine the degree of success a quasi-experimental design was utilized with a control group of regular probationers selected as a comparison. The findings from this study indicate that, while the experimental group reported slightly more criminal activity, there were no significant differences between the groups with regard to recidivism or social adjustment. Data from the study also suggested that, although the program was clearly supervising high risk cases, the level of contacts and services was below program objectives, and certainly less than what should be provided high risk felony probationers.

* An earlier version of this paper was presented at the annual meeting of the Academy of Criminal Justice Sciences in Orlando, Florida, March 1986.

INTRODUCTION

The recent increases in prison crowding have led to new and innovative alternatives to incarceration. With prison populations and construction costs at an all-time high, many jurisdictions have turned to intensive supervision. States such as Georgia, New Jersey, and Texas have developed and implemented programs statewide. Other states have encouraged, and in some instances funded, local programs. One such state is Ohio.

In 1978 Ohio made available subsidy monies for local probation departments to help reduce prison commitment rates, enabling the Lucas County (Toledo) Adult Probation Department to develop the Incarceration Diversion Unit (IDU). The primary goal of this program was to provide intensive supervision to offenders *after* they had been sentenced to a state penal institution. Unlike previous experiments with intensive supervision, the focus of this program was on the reduction of the local prison commitment rate. Through nearly six years of operation this program has reduced the county's commitment rate by 15.8 percent, and has saved the state approximately $2.2 million. (The IDU has been evaluated six times, and the results generally have been favorable. For the most recent, see Latessa, 1985). The success of the IDU has led the state to expand the concept throughout the largest counties in Ohio. In 1983, expansion of the state subsidy prompted the Lucas County Adult Probation Department to establish a unit devoted solely to the supervision of probationers classified as "high risk."

The purpose of this study is to examine the effectiveness of providing such increased contacts and services to a group of high risk probationers. In order to measure the effects of this treatment, a number of outcome indicators were examined, including recidivism and positive adjustment. A control group was selected from the balance of the IDU's caseload and matched according to several variables.

ISSUES IN INTENSIVE SUPERVISION

While there has been a great deal of interest and research on the effects of intensive supervision (Robinson, Wilkins, Carter and Wahl, 1969; Gottfredson and Neithercutt, 1974; Sasfy, 1975; Banks, Porter, Rardin, Siler and Unger, 1976; Fallen, Apperson, Holt-Milligan and Roe, 1981), much of this effort has been of questionable value (Adams and Vetter, 1971; Latessa, 1979; Fields, 1984). The three major issues surrounding the use of intensive supervision have been the effectiveness question; the caseload size and classification issue; and the debate over the number and quality of contacts.

The question of effectiveness has gone largely unanswered. There appears to be some success with "specially" selected offenders (Banks, Porter, Rardin, Siler and Unger, 1977; Latessa and Vito, 1984), but overall anticipated reductions in recidivism have not materialized.

As far as caseload size, experiments with intensive supervision have resulted in lower numbers of offenders per officer, with the average caseload around twenty-five. The crucial operational issue has been the accuracy of selection of cases appropriate for higher levels of supervision. The most widely used screening techniques involve risk and/or needs assessment instruments (Baird, 1983).

As expected, the number of contacts with clients has increased under intensive supervision, but the question of whether "intensity" should simply involve increasing the number of contacts still remains. The average number of contacts for cases under intensive supervision has been about four per month, compared to about one per month under "regular" supervision. This difference in contact levels has not invoked a sense of "intense" supervision. Recently, Georgia and New Jersey have instituted intensive supervision programs that assign two officers caseloads of ten, with contacts required at least daily (Bennett, 1984). It appears, however, that the primary purpose of these contacts is surveillance, not treatment. It also appears that clients in these programs are provided this level of supervision for a much shorter time than in many of the traditional intensive supervision programs. It should also be noted that both of these states have centralized state probationer services. It is unlikely that local probation departments could provide the same level of service in a cost effective manner.

The present study adds to this base of knowledge by comparing the performance of high risk probationers placed in intensive supervision versus probationers placed on regular supervision. The key issue is whether intensive supervision, through improved service delivery, can have an impact upon high risk probationers, and thus serve as a basis for programs to divert similar offenders from overcrowded penal facilities.

HIGH RISK UNIT

In July 1983, the probation subsidy grant mentioned above was renewed with the Ohio Department of Rehabilitation and Correction. Included in the agreement was the development of a high risk program within the original IDU. Part of this contract was a commitment by the probation department to implement the Case Management System (CMS) by the end of calendar year 1983. This system allows the classification of offenders into three risk levels: high, medium, and low. (The risk and needs assessment instruments were developed by the U.S. National Institute of Corrections and are widely used as part of the model case management system.) The assumption was that high risk offenders need proportionately more probation resources, especially probation officer time.

The program employed three probation officers, each assigned a maximum of 50 cases. The officers were required to make at least two face-to-face contacts per month, and to verify client employment and residence. Cases selected for the unit were all classified by the intake unit of the department. A total of 172 felony probationers were supervised between July 1983 and July 1985. An additional 60 cases were placed into the unit after March 1985, but they were not included in this study due to the relatively short period of follow-up.

RESEARCH METHODS

A quasi-experimental design was utilized, with a comparison group matched and selected from the balance of the department's caseload. The primary matching variables included sex, race, and, when possible, risk level. Shock probationers admitted to the high risk unit were matched, when possible, with shock probationers assigned to the regular caseloads. (In Ohio, offenders may be eligible for early release from prison under shock probation; see Vito, 1978.) Comparison cases were under supervision during the same time period and for a similar length of time as the experimental group. This insured that the cases were at least similar on some basic parameters.

Data for this study were collected from the agency's files. Information on the clients under supervision covered a one year period, from July 1984 to July 1985. Since this is an ongoing program, only those cases admitted before March 1985 were included in this evaluation. A total of 172 experimental cases and 133 comparison cases comprised the samples. The difference in sample sizes was due to the fact that comparison cases were not always available. After information on the two samples was gathered, it was divided into two basic types: in-program and outcome.

In-program data were designed to examine the differences between the two groups at program entry, and to measure the level of service delivery provided the clients. In-program data included information on background characteristics, risk and needs assessment, and the number and types of contacts and services provided.

The outcome measures were designed to examine whether or not intensive supervision had an impact on high risk probationers. The outcome indicators included recidivism (operationally defined as incarceration in a penal institution), and secondary measures of criminal behavior including arrests, convictions, and technical violations.

In addition to the above, the severity of criminal offenses and the rate of social adjustment were measured through the use of a relative adjustment index. This index, which was developed and validated by researchers at the Program for the Study of Crime and Delinquency at Ohio State University, has been used in diverse settings, including institutional drug-alcohol programs, reintegration centers and adult halfway houses. The first part of the relative adjustment scale is a continuous measure of criminal behavior based upon severity of offenses as delineated by the Ohio Revised Code. The second part of the index represents a positive adjustment scale which includes factors related to employment, education, residential and financial situation and progress on probation. These two scales were separately analyzed to determine the severity of criminal behavior (for new convictions), and to measure any advances in social adjustment.

RESULTS

In-Program Analysis

The primary purpose of the in-program analysis was to measure the differences between the two groups on background variables, and the extent of contacts and service delivery.

With regard to the matching variables race and sex, the two groups were almost identical. Males far outnumbered females, and blacks slightly outnumbered whites. There were no differences in "marital status," "other family criminality," "veteran of military" or "on drugs or alcohol during current offense." The remaining factors, however, did indicate significant differences between the two groups. The high risk group was slightly older, less educated and had fewer jobs during the past five years than the comparison group. It was not surprising that the risk and needs classification data were significant. Nearly 94 percent of the experimental group were classified as high risk and 87.8 percent evidenced high needs. This compared to 27 percent high risk and 28.6 percent high needs for the control group. Finally, there was a significant difference in employment, with only 16.4 percent of the experimental group employed at entry versus 29.7 percent of the comparison group.

The data on criminal justice history also revealed statistically significant differences between the two samples. The high risk group had been on probation more often, had more prior personal offenses, had been incarcerated more often and longer, and had more prior convictions and total number of arrests. They also had been first arrested at a younger age. The only factor that was not statistically significant was age at first conviction. These findings support the contention that the experimentals comprised an extremely high risk group in need of special attention.

The final background factors concerned special problems at program entry. The experimental group had significantly more alcohol abuse, psychiatric history, and prior drug and alcohol treatment. Again, these data are indicative of a high risk, high needs group.

In order to examine the level of service provision, data were gathered on the types of services provided during the first year of operation. The experimental group received a significantly higher level of mental health and welfare services, and a significantly lower level of group and individual counseling. In all of the remaining areas (vocational, educational, employment, drug, alcohol and family counseling), the high risk group received a higher level of service, but the differences were not significant.

Another critical question pertained to the number of contacts with the high risk cases. The data on contacts made by the probation officers in each group are presented in Table 1. Contacts were divided into four categories: face-to-face in the office, face-to-face in other locales, collateral and total contacts. These data indicated that the experimental group received significantly more face-to-face other, collateral and total contacts. Overall, the high risk group received 2.58 contacts per month compared to 1.63 for the comparison group. The experimental group received slightly less (1.46) than their goal of two face-to-face contacts per month.

Table 1

Monthly Probation Contacts
(July 1984 Through July 1985)

Group	Type of Contact			
	Face to Face Office	Face to Face Other*	Collateral*	Total*
Experimental	.81	.65	1.21	2.58
Comparison	.92	.09	.62	1.63

*Significant at .05 level

Table 2

Arrests, Convictions and Technical Violations Filed

Variable	Experimental		Comparison	
	N	%	N	%
Misdemeanor Arrests	82	29.0	26	17.3
Misdemeanor Convictions*	63	25.0	25	11.2
Felony Arrests	42	17.4	18	11.3
Felony Convictions	26	13.4	16	9.7
Technical Violations	71	17.4	30	12.7
Probation Violations	28	15.6	28	12.8

*Significant at .05 level. N is based on the total number of offenses, while the percentages are based upon the actual number of cases reporting violations.

Outcome Analysis

In order to examine the criminal activity of these two groups while under supervision, arrest, conviction, and technical violations were considered. As demonstrated in Table 2, the only significant difference was in misdemeanor convictions, with 25 percent of the experimental group versus 11.2 percent of the comparison group reporting convictions. The experimental group had slightly more misdemeanor and felony arrests, felony convictions and technical violations, but the differences were not significant. The two groups reported the same number of probation violations.

Table 3 presents the status of the experimental and comparison samples at the end of the evaluation period. The two groups were similar with regard to the proportions of clients still on probation, absconding, and revoked. The comparison group had slightly fewer clients incarcerated for felonies and misdemeanors, but these differences were not significant. The only significant difference was in the number of offenders released from probation. The comparison group reported 15 percent released, as opposed to 6.9 percent for the high risk group. The major indicator of failure—incarceration in a penal institution—was determined by combining the probation revoked and incarcerated group with the incarcerated felony group. Though 20.3 percent of the experimental group was incarcerated—compared to 13.4 percent of the control group—this difference was not significant.

Designed to measure the severity of offenses as prescribed by the Ohio Revised Code, the criminal behavior severity scale is continuous, with a range from -11 for aggravated murder to -.5 for technical violation (see Table 4). This scale is additive and permits measurement over time. The total weighted scores for each group are presented in Table 5. The overall mean score for the experimental group was -2.27, compared to -1.54 for the control group. This difference was not significant. Though it appears that the experimental group was convicted of new offenses that were slightly more severe, overall the difference was not significant.

Table 3

Current Status of the
Experimental and Comparison Group

	Experimental		Control	
	N	%	N	%
Status				
Released from Probation*	12	6.9	20	15.0
On Probation	99	57.5	79	59.3
Probation Revoked and Incarcerated	14	8.1	9	6.7
Incarcerated Felony	21	12.2	9	6.7
Incarcerated Misdemeanor	5	2.9	0	0.0
Absconded	12	6.9	9	6.7
Transferred	2	1.1	1	.8
Revoked, Placed in Another Unit	3	1.7	4	3.0
Other	4	2.3	2	1.5
	172	100.0	133	100.0

*Significant at .05 level.

Table 4

Criminal Behavior Severity Scale

Degree of Offense	Assigned Score
Aggravated Murder	—11
Murder	—10
Felony 1st	— 9
Felony 2nd	— 8
Felony 3rd	— 7
Felony 4th	— 6
Misdemeanor 1st	— 5
Misdemeanor 2nd	— 4
Misdemeanor 3rd	— 3
Misdemeanor 4th	— 2
Minor Misdemeanor	— 1
Violator at Large	— 1
Technical Violation	— 0.5
Probation Violation	— 0.5

Table 5

Criminal Behavior Severity

Group	Total Score	Mean	F	Significance	N
Experimental	—381	—2.27			168
			3.7	N.S.	
Control	—205	—1.54			133

Table 6

Positive Adjustment Scale

Assigned Score	Adjustment Criterion
+1	Employed, enrolled in school, or participating in a training program for more than 50 percent of the follow-up period.
+1	Held any one job (or continued in educational or vocational program) for more than six months during the follow-up.
+1	Attained vertical mobility in employment, educational, or vocational program.
+1	For the last half of follow-up period, individual was self-supporting and supported any immediate family.
+1	Individual shows stability in residency. Either lived in the same residence for more than six months or moved at suggestion or with the agreement of supervising officer.
+1	Individual has avoided any critical incidents that show instability, immaturity, or inability to solve problems acceptably.
+1	Attainment of financial stability. This is indicated by the individual living within his means, opening bank accounts, or meeting debt payments.
+1	Participation in self-improvement programs. These could be vocational, educational, group counseling, alcohol or drug maintenance programs.
+1	Individual making satisfactory progress through probation period. This could be moving downward in levels of supervision or obtaining final release within period.
+1	No illegal activities on any available records during the follow-up period.

The positive adjustment scale is designed to measure several parameters generally considered to demonstrate "acceptable societal behavior." These items are presented in Table 6. The total scores are presented in Table 7 and are based on measures taken at the end of the evaluation period. The mean score for the high risk group was 3.6, compared to 4.3 for the comparison group. This difference was significant, with the comparison group having made a better social adjustment than the experimental group.

Table 7

Positive Adjustment Results

Group	Total Score	Mean	F	Significance	N
Experimental	610	3.6			172
			25.9	.00	
Control	561	4.3			130

SUMMARY AND CONCLUSIONS

This study has examined the effects of intensive supervision with high risk probationers. As a result of this study, a number of tentative conclusions can be reached.

First, despite attempts to match the two groups, it was obvious that a number of significant differences existed. The experimental group had much more prior involvement with the criminal justice system. While the differences were statistically controlled, the fact remains that these offenders were the worst the department had to offer. The experimental group also had more special problems, but again, this is indicative of a high risk/needs group.

The data on services are perhaps the most puzzling. While the experimental group received more services overall, and significantly more in the area of mental health and welfare, they also received significantly less family and individual counseling. Clearly this is a group in need of substantial assistance in employment, education and substance abuse, yet the data suggest that sufficient services were not provided.

Though the experimental group was receiving significantly more contacts, the number of face-to-face contacts was below the program goal. Again, these data suggest that more "high quality" contacts need to be made in order for this program to justify the label "intensive supervision."

The outcome indicators suggest that the high risk group held its own. Overall, the high risk group had 20.3 percent incarcerated, compared to 13.4 percent for the control group, but this difference was not significant. Indeed, given the high risk nature of the experimental group, one might expect them to do significantly worse (Travis, 1984).

The criminal behavior severity scale revealed that the high risk sample had committed offenses no more serious then the comparison group. This is an important finding since it indicates that the high risk sample posed no more threat to the community than regular probationers.

The positive adjustment scale did uncover a significant difference, with the comparison group making a better social adjustment than the experimental group. While this finding is disappointing, it is not surprising given the host of problems faced by, and prior records of the high risk group.

There are several plausible explanations for these findings. First, despite the attempts at matching a comparison group, important differences remained. Although these differences were controlled statistically, the experimental group still represented the worst cases the department had to supervise. Given the high risk nature of this group, it is highly unlikely that an adequate comparison group can be developed from the remaining cases in the department. Another problem was the relatively short duration of treatment and follow-up. As mentioned previously, this is an ongoing program and a more extensive follow-up will be conducted at a later date.

It is also possible that intensive supervision with high risk probationers is not feasible, and that even with reduced caseloads and increased contacts not enough time can be devoted to these offenders. On the other hand, it is also likely that these offenders would not have done as well had they not received additional attention. The fact that the vast majority of the department's high risk cases were no longer being supervised by regular probation officers may have increased the success rate of these non-intensive caseloads, since these officers did not have to deal with the most difficult cases. It should also be reiterated that the experimental group's performance was not significantly different with regard to the major indicators of recidivism.

Finally, the data indicate that this program did not operate as an ideal example of intensive supervision, certainly not at the level of some of the "new generation" programs such as Georgia's and New Jersey's. Available research never has demonstrated conclusively that intensive supervision affects recidivism. However, there appears to be mounting evidence that we can divert high risk/need offenders from prison without seriously jeopardizing community safety. Whether or not these offenders would be acceptable to community supervision without the guise of intensive supervision has not been determined. It is hoped that future research will help answer some of these questions.

REFERENCES

Adams, R. and H.J. Vetter (1971). "Effectiveness of Probation Caseload Sizes: A Review of the Empirical Literature." *Criminology* 9: 333-343.

Baird, C. (1983). "Probation and Parole Classification: The Wisconsin Model." In: *Classification as a Management Tool: Theories and Models for Decisionmakers,* edited by the American Correctional Association, College Park, MD.

Banks, J., A.L. Porter, R.L. Rardin, T.R. Siler, and V.E. Unger (1976). *Issue Paper: Phase I Evaluation of Intensive Special Probation Project.* Atlanta, GA: School of Industrial and System Engineering, Georgia Institute of Technology.

————and A.L. Porter, R.L. Rardin, T.R. Siler and V.E. Unger (1977). *Summary, Phase I Evaluation of Intensive Probation Projects.* Washington, DC: U.S. Government Printing Office.

Bennett, L. (1984). "Practice in Search of Theory: The Case of Intensive Supervision." Paper presented at the annual meeting of the Academy of Criminal Justice Sciences, Chicago, IL.

Fallen, D., C. Apperson, J. Holt-Milligan, and J. Roe (1981). *Intensive Parole Supervision.* Olympia, WA: Dept. of Social and Health Services, Analysis and Information Service Division, Office of Research.

Fields, C.B. (1984). *The Intensive Supervision Probation Program in Texas: A Two Year Assessment.* Unpublished doctoral dissertation. Huntsville, TX: Sam Houston State University.

Gottfredson, D. and M. Neithercutt (1974). *Caseload Size Variation and Difference in Probation/Parole Performance.* Pittsburgh, PA: National Center for Juvenile Justice.

Latessa, E.J. (1979). *Intensive Supervision: An Evaluation of the Effectiveness of an Intensive Diversion Unit.* Unpublished doctoral dissertation. Columbus, OH: Ohio State University.

————(1985). *The Incarceration Diversion Unit of the Lucas County Adult Probation Department Report Number Six.* Department of Criminal Justice, Univ. of Cincinnati.

————and G. Vito (1984). "The Effects of Intensive Supervision on Shock Probationers." Paper presented at the Annual Meeting of the Academy of Criminal Justice Sciences, Chicago, IL.

Robinson, J., L.T. Wilkins, R. Carter, and A. Wahl (1969). *The San Francisco Project: A Study of Federal Probation and Parole.* Univ. of California at Berkeley: School of Criminology.

Sasfy, Joseph H. (1975). *An Experimentation of Intensive Supervision as a Treatment Strategy for Probationers.* National Level Evaluation Final Report. Washington, DC: Mitre Corp.

Travis, L. (1984). "Intensive Supervision in Probation and Parole." *Corrections Today* 46(4): 34-40.

Vito, Gennaro (1978). *Shock Probation in Ohio: A Comparison of Attributes and Outcome.* Unpublished doctoral dissertation. Columbus, OH: Ohio State University.

A Reassessment of Intensive Service Probation*

by
Lawrence A. Bennett

The initial analysis of an NIJ-funded study on intensive service supervision revealed that with more thorough initial diagnosis and careful classification probationers could be grouped on the basis of levels of service required to provide for control and social/emotional needs. Such a classification and service delivery system, while not leading to reduced recidivism, did lead to improvements in social adjustment indicators, including employment. With the use of the classification approaches suggested, some probationers were easily identified as requiring minimal levels of supervision, releasing resources to be used with more difficult cases. With this reallocation of resources, probation services could be more effectively delivered without increases in costs. Because the findings were based on a total sample of males, females, felons and misdemeanants, it was felt that more significant findings might be masked. However, findings based upon analysis of male felon cases

* While the reanalysis of this study was conducted under the auspices of the U.S. National Institute of Justice, the views expressed are those of the author and do not necessarily reflect the official position of the National Institute of Justice or the U.S. Department of Justice. The author is indebted for the data analysis functions performed by Brian Weisema of the University of Maryland under a contract from the National Institute of Justice.

113

*only reflected results very similar to those for the sample as a whole—
namely, improved ratings in social adjustment measures without a
reduction in recidivism. Possible reasons for the findings are explored.*

Despite the fact that probation and probation with jail represent the most
common dispositions of convicted offenders, questions have been raised
as to the appropriateness of these procedures, especially with felony offenders (Petersilia, Turner, Kahan and Peterson, 1985). With prison
populations ranging well above rated capacities, a number of dispositional
alternatives are being examined. Within this framework, "regular" probation continues to be a mainstay among the sentences available. At the
same time, there seems to be a relative dearth of experimental studies
to guide practitioners toward improving probation in field applications.

In the mid-1970s the U.S. National Institute of Justice awarded a grant
to evaluate the then current situation in probation, with emphasis on
special projects and intensive supervision. The resulting study (Banks,
Porter, Rardin, Siler and Unger, 1977) noted that while there were a
number of innovative approaches being tried in the field, almost none
had been subjected to critical evaluation. It was from this preliminary overview that the current study was developed (Romm 1982). Researchers
selected several potential participant jurisdictions and assisted their personnel in developing experimental project proposals designed to test key
elements in the probation process. From this array, the best project was
chosen for further refinement and complete development for the study,
with assistance in implementation. The implementation was followed by
a detailed and thorough evaluation.

The evaluation design chosen addressed two issues: the classification
of clientele and differing levels of service delivery. A review of promising approaches to probation supervision (Nelson, Olemart and Harlow,
1978) noted that improved classification systems were essential to determine both control requirements and treatment needs if staff time were
to be more appropriately allocated. In this study, the classification system,
developed by the Wisconsin Bureau of Community Corrections in 1975,
was called the Client Management Classification (CMC) system. CMC involves a structured interview procedure that leads to a relatively objective assessment of the client's requirements for social services and control, and categorizes each client into one of four case management treatment strategies.

A number of prior research efforts (Adams, 1967; Adams and Vetter,
1971; Banks, Porter, Rardin, Siler and Unger, 1977; Baird, 1983) suggest

that the results of increasing contacts have mixed results. To some extent the unclear outcomes occur because higher rates of technical violations may obscure any gains from increased treatment. In spite of these earlier difficulties, the present study was designed to place increased emphasis on improved case management both through a structured diagnostic approach and a more systematic mobilization of support services, all planned to more adequately meet both the control and treatment needs of the probationers.

Four hypotheses were generated:

1. Utilization of the CMC system will provide more effective application of services and probationer rehabilitation than is provided by currently employed diagnostic and planning procedures.

2. Implementation of a system of broadly differentiated levels of service intensity will enhance the economic and therapeutic effectiveness of the probation system over levels of cost and service benefit achieved using the existing treatment modality.

3. For high risk probationers, an initial six month period of intensive service will result in more positive probation outcomes.

4. For lowest risk probationers, limited service probation will be as effective as normal probation supervision.

Methodology

The study population, drawn from a regional office of a state probation program that processed over 2,500 offenders per year, was assigned to eight test groups on the basis of risk/needs assessment and random assignment. On the basis of risk assessment ratings, three levels of risk were designated: low, medium and high. Those rated as high risk were placed in one group, while the low and medium risk probationers were structured into a second group. Each major group was then randomly divided on the basis of odd/even case numbers with even-numbered cases receiving the Client Management Classification (CMC) system interviews. For high risk probationers, each subgroup was further divided on the basis of random assignment into two groups—one to receive intensive service supervision for the first six months before transfer to a normal supervision unit, while the second group would be placed under regular supervision from the start.

Those rated as low/medium risk were divided on a random basis into those receiving CMC interviews and those not interviewed. The subgroups were further divided into those receiving normal supervision and those given limited service levels of supervision. Assignment to limited service groups was not on a random basis, however. Rather, the assignment was based upon low risk/low needs scores for those without the CMC interview, and others classified as Selected Intervention (SI) for those interviewed by the CMC process.

Figure 1 outlines the flow of probationers into the various groups.

The Special Service Supervision Approach

The program to enhance both the quality and frequency of interaction between agents and the probationers was designated as *Intensive Service Supervision*. Prominent aspects include the use of extensive case histories, involvement of supervisors and other agents in reviewing comprehensive service plans, and obtaining input of vendor personnel in the development of the integrated service plan. Probation officers were encouraged to refer family members for needed supportive services with the aim of improving the home environment for the client. Home visits by the agent were encouraged and monthly verification of residence and employment was required, along with face-to-face treatment sessions once every two weeks. Collateral contacts were conducted as necessary, and the clients were required to complete a monthly report. (Figure 2 provides an overview of how Intensive Service Supervision differed from regular supervision and the limited intervention.) For those receiving limited supervision, the single requirement was the submission of a monthly report. Any contacts between the client and the probation department would be initiated by the client except for incidents related to law violations.

Measures Employed

Procedure. Information used in the study was either recorded by the probation officer or extracted from official files and entered into a computerized system. Data analyses were conducted by extracting data from the automated system.

Process. To document what actually transpired during the experimental process, the number and kind of contacts between probation agents and their clients were recorded. In addition, the number and type of referrals were incorporated. Thus, in the two areas the measures were as follows:

• Probation agents' activities—direct client contact; and collateral phone and mail contacts with the probationer.

• Referrals—number of referrals, types of referrals, and agent's assessment of clients' use of referrals.

Figure 1

Probationer Flow to Test Groups

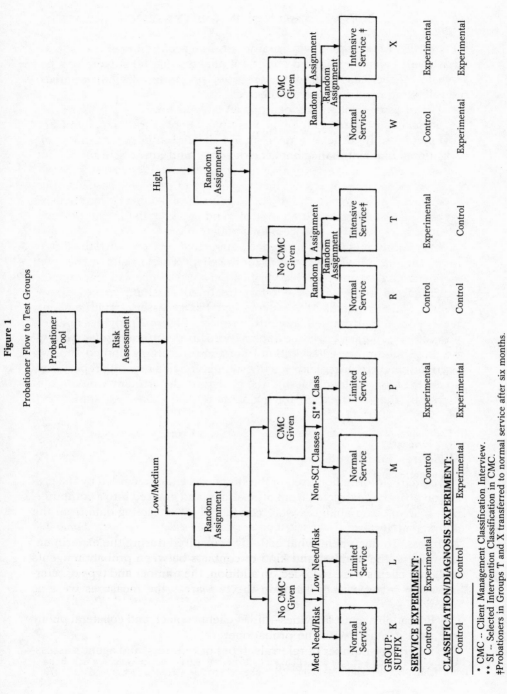

* CMC -- Client Management Classification Interview.
** SI -- Selected Intervention Classification in CMC.
‡Probationers in Groups T and X transferred to normal service after six months.

Outcome Measures. Two major areas—recidivism and social adjustment—were considered important in assessing the outcome of the provision of services as part of the probation program. Within these areas the following measures were collected:

• Recidivism—probation violations and revocations.

• Social Adjustment—employment status (school or training), living arrangement/family structure, drug and/or alcohol abuse, repayment of obligations/financial management, risk score, and needs score.

Figure 2

Comparison of Service Delivery Modes[1]

Activity	Modes		
	Intensive	**Normal**	**Limited**
I. Staffing			
a. Staff involvement	Agent, Supervisor, Other agents	Agent	Agent
b. Depth of social history	Extensive	Average	Little
c. Involvement of vendors	Yes	No	No
II. Verification of employment, residence	Once per month	Once per month	Once
III. Monitoring and review			
a. Supervisor audit	Routine	No	No
b. Review procedure	Group restaff per non-report, major violation	Ad hoc agent review	Early dismissal review
IV. Home involvement	Environmental assessment, referral	As necessary	As necessary
V. Frequency of face-to-face contact	Once every 2 weeks	1 per month or every 2 weeks	Once every 3 months
VI. Monthly written reports	Yes	Yes	Yes

[1]Modified from chart presented in "Plan for an Experimental Project in Probation Rehabilitation," Chase Riveland and Marianne A. Cooke, Wisconsin Division of Corrections, 1979.

Sample

Rather than a random sample, a total population was chosen made up of adult offenders sentenced to probation January 1980 through June 1981, less several excluded categories. Excluded probation categories were:

• Juvenile cases—the experiment was limited to adult probationers.

• Non-residents of Milwaukee County—not available to receive local services, as their probation cases were transferred to the county of residence.

• Those already on probation when convicted of the new current offense—already being provided normal services.

• Severe psychotic or severe sex-deviate cases—not suitable for the experimental design.

• Jail-work release sentences of more than ten days followed by probation.

• Those probationers who were "no-shows"; i.e., who 'did not report to probation intake after sentencing, and were immediate absconders.

.The work release category resulted in the largest number being excluded from the experiment.

The resulting sample of 1,882 probationers was made up of 28 percent felons and 72 percent misdemeanants; 20 percent were female. Black and white groups were equal at 48 percent. Over 27 percent had one or more prior felony convictions, with slightly over 50 percent showing neither prior felony nor misdemeanor convictions. One in seven offenders was categorized as having high needs. Slightly more than one-third were employed full time, with an additional eight or nine percent employed part-time. Nearly half of the sample (49.4 percent) were considered high risk; less than one-third were classified as low risk (28.2 percent). Over half were below age 24 (54.4 percent).

Need for Reanalysis of the Data

Because preliminary analyses suggested that the subpopulations within the total sample were similar in several attributes, it was felt that the population could be treated as a single entity for analytic purposes. However, futher analyses might be valuable for a number of reasons. First, historically the criminal justice system has responded differentially to women; thus, use of a combined sample might mask valuable insights. Second, felony probation is of greater social concern than misdemeanor probation and therefore should be considered separately. Also the probation agents supervising cases might well exercise greater control over the felony cases because of the more serious nature of the offenses, and therefore the intervention "treatment" might be stronger.

Findings From the Initial Analysis

A number of questions can be addressed based upon findings from the initial analysis. The first of these is, does the introduction of intensive probation services affect the probation outcome of high risk probationers? The answer must be "no." The rates of successful completions, revocations, new offenses and absconders were no different for those provided with intensive service from those receiving normal service (see Table 1).

Table 1

Probation Performance Outcomes
Experimental Period
January 1980 — June 1981
by Risk and Service Level[1]

	Risk and Service Level			
Risk Level:	**Low/Medium**			**High**
Service Level:	Limited	Normal	Normal	Intensive
N:	481	491	350	428
Outcome	**(percent of total group)**			
Successful Completion	23.1	13.0	19.4	12.2
Continue under Supervision	74.4	81.1	70.6	78.3
Revoked - Total	2.1	4.9	10.0	6.5
New Convictions[2]	1.0	1.6	6.3	2.6
Charge/Arrested[3]	0.8	1.6	2.6	1.6
Absconded	0.2	1.0	0.6	2.1
Rule Violation	0.0	0.6	0.6	0.2
Other[4]	0.4	1.0	0.0	3.0

[1]Extrapolated from Exhibits III-C-1, 2 and 3 (Romm, 1982).
[2]Includes convictions of a new offense, or revocation in lieu of a new conviction.
[3]Includes charged but not yet convicted, or arrested but not charged.
[4]Includes deaths and transfers to other jurisdictions.

Question 2. "Did intensive service make any difference in outcome?" Here the answer is quite positive. While recidivism was not affected, intensive service probationers performed significantly better than their high risk counterparts receiving normal service on all indicators of *social adjustment* (see Table 2).

Table 2

Living Adjustment Indicators
Initial vs. Reassessment Distributions
by Service Level Comparison Groups
January 1980 — June 1981[1]

	COMPARISON SETS							
Groups:	L + P		K + M		T + X		R + W	
Service Level:	Limited		Normal		Intensive		Normal	
I/R*	I	R	I	R	I	R	I	R
N =	296		294		253		222	
INDICATOR	*(percent of total)*							
Total Needs Scores								
Low	82.1	86.0	39.7	47.2	35.6	51.8	37.1	42.1
Medium	16.5	13.3	47.6	40.3	43.5	30.0	47.1	43.4
High	1.4	0.7	12.7	12.4	20.9	18.2	15.8	14.5
Marital/Family Relations								
Relatively Stable	77.5	84.6	43.3	42.3	41.1	45.5	30.2	36.0
Some Disorganization	20.4	13.3	37.9	40.3	39.5	40.7	47.3	45.5
Major Disorganization	2.1	2.1	18.8	17.4	19.4	13.8	22.5	18.5
Address Changes (in last 12 months)								
None	57.0	58.6	50.2	49.8	42.3	44.5	45.0	42.8
One	32.2	27.5	25.6	31.1	33.0	29.5	32.8	32.3
Two or More	10.8	13.9	24.2	19.1	24.7	26.0	22.2	24.9
Alcohol Abuse								
No Interference with Functioning	84.8	98.3	62.9	90.4	49.4	85.5	46.1	77.2
Occasional Abuse	12.5	1.7	27.9	8.5	28.6	14.1	32.2	22.8
Frequent Abuse	2.7	0.0	9.2	1.1	22.0	0.4	21.7	0.0
Drug Abuse								
No Interference with Functioning	85.5	95.3	70.2	81.3	74.5	65.7	72.0	62.4
Occasional Abuse	12.6	4.4	24.6	17.6	16.2	20.3	22.2	18.0
Frequent Abuse	2.0	0.3	5.2	1.1	9.3	14.0	5.8	19.6
Emotional Stability								
No Symptoms	93.0	93.7	61.1	63.1	61.7	64.4	59.9	60.8
Symptoms Limit Functioning	7.0	6.0	30.4	29.4	29.6	28.5	34.7	32.4
Symptoms Prohibit Functioning	0.0	0.3	3.5	7.5	8.7	7.1	5.4	6.8
Probation Officers' Impression of Probationers' Needs								
Low	62.8	67.0	10.2	14.6	11.1	30.4	11.8	18.1
Medium	33.0	26.7	51.0	50.7	33.2	33.6	43.4	40.7
High	4.2	6.3	38.8	34.7	55.7	36.0	44.8	41.2

*I = initial assessment at admission
 R = reassessment after first six months or at termination of probation.

[1]Represents a copy of Exhibit III-C-5 (Romm, 1982).

Question 3. "Were intensive service probationers treated differently from those subjected to normal supervision? Again, we find that those under intensive service did receive an increased level of service. During the period of intensive service, probationers received more face-to-face and phone contacts than those high risk probationers receiving normal service (see Table 3). In addition, intensive service probationers were referred more frequently and were more often referred to higher levels of social and community service agencies (see Table 4).

Table 3

Probation Officer Contacts - First Six Months of Probation

Experimental and Control Groups
by Service Level[1]
(N = 1750)

Risk and Service Level

Groups:	**Low/Medium Risk**		**High Risk**	
Service Level:	Limited	Normal	Normal	Intensive
N:	481	491	350	428
CONTACT TYPE	(Average number of contacts)			
Face-to-Face: Total	3.14	7.24	8.72	9.76
with Probationer	2.87	6.15	7.43	8.42
Collateral	.27	1.09	1.29	1.34
Phone: Total	2.22	7.33	8.30	10.13
with Probationer	1.18	2.95	3.08	3.51
Collateral	1.04	4.38	5.22	6.62
Mail: Total	3.65	2.50	2.52	2.25
with Probationer	2.68	1.21	1.40	1.43
Collateral	.97	1.29	1.12	.82
All: Total	9.01	17.07	19.54	22.14
with Probationer	6.73	10.31	11.91	13.36
Collateral	2.28	6.76	7.63	8.78

[1]Adapted from Exhibit III -B-5 (Romm, 1982).

Table 4

Referral Patterns
First Six Months of Probation
by Risk Service Level[1]

	Risk and Service Level			
Risk Level:	**Low/Medium**		**High**	
Service Level:	*Limited*	*Normal*	*Normal*	*Intensive*
Probationers Referred (Number)	92	105	78	128
Percent of Total	28.9	33.3	36.8	50.8
Percent of Probationers Referred for:				
Diagnostic Assistance	10.9	30.5	39.7	24.2
Mental Health, Alcoholism and Drug Abuse Treatment	23.9	67.6	76.9	40.6
Vocational Training/Job Assistance	58.7	51.4	34.6	40.6
Educational Training	5.4	13.3	12.8	10.9
Welfare Assistance	0.0	10.5	5.1	8.6
Developmental Disability	1.1	1.0	1.3	0.8

[1]Adapted from Exhibit III-B-10 (Romm, 1982).

Question 4. "Did the use of the CMC diagnostic interview affect outcome?" There was no evidence that the availability of the CMC interviewers or the use of CMC diagnostics influenced the results.

Question 5. "Were the high risk candidates really the right target group?" Generally speaking "yes," with the group made up of those classed as "clearly high risk, having a larger proportion with social service needs, high unemployment rates and significantly earlier criminal histories" (Romm, 1982: 235). However, at the same time, a large fraction of the high risk probationers were classified by CMC as falling into the "Selective Intervention" category, suggesting a need for only limited service. This apparently comes about because the need/risk assessment puts great weight on prior assaultive offenses, often associated with a positive potential for adjustment under supervision and an absence of social service problems.

Question 6. "How did limited service probationers do?" Very well. This group had the highest rate of successful completions and the lowest rate of revocations, new offenses and absconders. It should be remembered that this group was selected either as "Selective Intervention" cases by the CMC approach or as low risk/need cases by the more usual classification technique. Those placed into the limited service category had a higher proportion of females, a higher employment rate, and a lower rate of prior criminal involvement, particularly indicating lower numbers of prior felonies.

Question 7. "How well do the two systems classify high and low risk offenders?" Here we have a mixed finding. The identification of a limited services pool seems quite simple. By either system much the same group would be selected, and, as can be seen from the characteristics outlined above as well as their probation adjustment, they are indeed low risk probationers. The identification of the high risk group, however, is not so straightforward. The usual risk/needs assessment process selected different people than did the CMC technique. At the same time, a number of people were selected who needed only minimal assistance of any sort.

Question 8. "Did the findings support the original hypotheses?" For the most part, "yes." By making use of limited service supervision for those representing low risk, resources were made available to provide more intensive service for those requiring intervention. Thus, the application of the *total process* led to a more effective application of services without increases in costs and without increased recidivism. The study provided additional support for the notion that a fair segment of a probation population can be identified for whom only minimal services need be provided while not in any way increasing the danger to society. What was not demonstrated was support for hypothesis number 3, that intensive service for high risk offenders would result in improved outcome. While significant improvement was noted in social adjustment indicators, recidivism remained unaffected.

Findings from the Reanalysis

An attempt was made to provide parallel analysis for male felons only to more clearly highlight differences that might occur. As in any process involving the remining of old tailings, not all data could be recovered in exactly the same format or extent as originally presented. In some situations, cases had to be eliminated because the coding did not fit available category definitions. In these instances it was assumed that the basis for difficulty was coder error, and that these errors would be distributed on a chance basis, thus not introducing a serious bias into the findings. In other situations, such as the reassessment of need levels, an estimate was made as to appropriate cutting points for low, medium and high need categories, since such specifications were not available in the original report. The result makes any comparison between male felons and the total sample questionable, but provides a rough guide to differences between the initial assessment and the reassessment for the male felon group, since the same cut-off points are used for both distributions.

When we look at the first and key question of whether intensive probation services change the probation outcome of high risk offenders, the answer drawn from the reassessment must be "no." The pattern for the male felons is much the same as for the group as a whole. Table 5 presents

Table 5

Male Felons Only
Probation Performance Outcomes
Experimental Period
January 1980 — June 1981
by Risk and Service Level

Risk and Service Level

Risk Level:	Low/Medium		High	
Service Level:	*Limited*	*Normal*	*Normal*	*Intensive*
N:	*90*	*129*	*96*	*109*
Outcome	(percent of total group)			
Successful Completion	11.1	3.1	1.0	2.8
Continue under Supervision	87.7	90.7	90.6	89.9
Revoked - Total	1.1	6.2	8.3	7.3
New Convictions[1]	1.1	2.3	4.2	5.5
Charge/Arrested[2]	0.0	2.3	1.0	.9
Absconded	0.0	.8	3.1	.9
Rule Violation	0.0	.8	0.0	0.0

[1]Includes convictions of a new offense, or revocation in lieu of a new conviction.
[2]Includes charged but not yet convicted, or arrested but not yet charged.

Table 6

Male Felons Only
Living Adjustment Indicators
Initial vs. Reassessment Distributions
by Service Level Comparison Groups
January 1980 — June 1981

	COMPARISON SETS							
Risk Level:	Low/Medium				High			
Service Level:	Limited		Normal		Intensive		Normal	
N =	64		42		60		52	
Assessment:[1]	I	R	I	R	I	R	I	R

INDICATOR *(percent of total)*

	I	R	I	R	I	R	I	R
Total Needs Scores								
Low	27.5	54.7	76.7	50.0	26.2	58.3	16.7	51.9
Medium	65.2	37.5	18.6	45.2	60.0	35.0	66.7	42.3
High	7.2	7.8	4.7	4.8	13.8	6.7	16.7	5.8
Marital/Family Relations								
Relatively Stable	45.2	57.5	78.7	55.3	45.5	60.6	29.1	45.5
Some Disorganization	41.1	28.8	17.0	31.9	40.9	24.2	52.7	41.8
Major Disorganization	13.7	13.7	4.3	12.8	13.6	15.3	18.2	12.7
Address Changes (in last 12 months)								
None	41.1	54.8	55.3	48.9	39.4	48.5	30.9	38.2
One	31.5	23.3	38.3	23.4	31.8	28.8	32.7	29.1
Two or More	27.4	21.9	6.4	27.7	28.8	22.7	36.4	32.7
Alcohol Abuse								
No Interference with Functioning	50.7	71.2	93.6	76.6	50.0	71.2	40.0	65.5
Occasional Abuse	38.4	23.3	2.1	12.8	34.9	19.7	40.0	23.9
Frequent Abuse	11.0	5.5	4.3	10.6	15.1	9.1	20.0	10.9
Drug Abuse								
No Interference with Functioning	64.4	82.2	78.7	78.7	69.7	86.4	61.8	72.7
Occasional Abuse	26.0	13.7	17.0	17.0	19.7	3.0	29.1	16.4
Frequent Abuse	9.6	4.1	4.3	4.3	10.6	10.6	9.1	10.9
Emotional Stability								
No Symptoms	68.5	75.3	85.1	70.2	77.3	77.3	65.5	72.7
Symptoms Limit Functioning	19.2	15.1	12.8	21.3	16.7	13.6	27.3	16.4
Symptoms Prohibit Functioning	12.3	9.6	2.1	8.5	6.1	9.1	7.3	10.9
Probation Officers' Impression of Probationers' Needs								
Low	5.5	31.5	63.8	31.9	7.6	30.3	5.5	29.1
Medium	50.7	48.0	25.5	44.7	37.9	43.9	29.1	38.2
High	43.8	20.5	10.6	23.4	54.6	25.8	65.5	32.7

[1] I and R stand for Initial and Reassessments.

the findings and, as can be seen, while those receiving intensive service had slightly fewer revocations and a few more successful completions, the differences are small and fall far short of statistical significance.

As to the effects of intensive service on outcomes, the results again parallel those of the total sample. While not reducing recidivism significantly, the living adjustment indicators all reflect positive shifts for those in the intensive service group, equal to or exceeding the positive gains made by those under normal supervision. Table 6 shows the initial and reassessment ratings for the living adjustment indicators.

Table 7

Probation Officer Contacts
First Six Months of Probation
by Risk and Service Level
Male Felons Only
(N = 387)

Risk and Service Level

Risk Level:	**Low/Medium Risk**		**High Risk**	
Service Level:	*Limited*	*Normal*	*Normal*	*Intensive*
N:	*81*	*121*	*80*	*105*
CONTACT TYPE	(Average number of contacts)			
Face-to-Face: Total	6.03	12.40	14.09	10.60
with Probationer	5.57	10.89	12.13	7.36
Collateral	.46	1.51	1.96	3.24
Phone: Total	4.37	10.68	13.56	17.83
with Probationer	1.72	3.82	5.08	5.15
Collateral	2.65	6.86	8.48	12.68
Mail: Total	5.82	4.00	3.51	3.27
with Probationer	4.50	1.81	1.68	1.54
Collateral	1.22	2.19	1.83	.1.73
All: Total	17.19	28.37	32.31	28.75
with Probation	12.70	17.31	19.60	12.04
Collateral	4.49	11.06	12.71	16.71

One must then ask the question, did those in the intensive service group receive different kinds of services from those under normal supervision? Here the picture is not so clear. Table 7 presents the number and kind of probation officer contacts with the male felons. It appears that the total number of contacts was lower during the treatment period for those receiving intensive service than for those under normal supervision. Even more serious, the average number of face-to-face contacts was considerably lower for the intensive service probationers. The only place where there is a marked difference in contacts favoring the intensive service group is in collateral phone contacts. This may be a reflection of the brokerage role the probation officer plays in the intensive service program, reflecting follow-up contacts with agencies to which probationers have been referred for service. However, it would not seem that this type of effort could compensate for the lower number of face-to-face contacts. Thus, questions could be raised as to whether the treatment planned was fully implemented in practice.

Table 8

Referral Patterns
First Six Months of Probation
by Risk and Service Level
Male Felons Only

Risk and Service Level

Risk Level:	**Low/Medium**		**High**	
Service Level:	Limited	Normal	Normal	Intensive
Probationers Referred:	19	27	13	19
Percent of Total	24.4	33.3	25.0	28.8
Percent of Probationers Referred for:				
Diagnostic Assistance	0.0	29.6	30.8	26.3
Mental Health, Alcoholism and Drug Abuse Treatment	26.3	66.6	89.3	52.6
Vocational Training/Job Assistance	73.7	55.5	46.2	42.1
Educational Training	10.5	11.1	7.7	10.5
Welfare Assistance	15.8	25.9	18.8	15.8

Along similar lines, Table 8, reflecting referral patterns, fails to indicate that those probationers under the intensive service program were referred much more frequently to specialized programs than those under normal supervision. There is a suggestion that high risk offenders under normal supervision had a somewhat heavier referral pattern than those in the intensive service group. Again, the question is raised as to the extent of impact of the planned treatment intervention.

The limited service groups again did considerably better in probation outcome, even among male felons only. They had more successful completions and fewer revocations. At the same time, their arrest and new conviction rates were far lower than for other groups.

DISCUSSION

It is now time to explain why reanalysis of the data failed to produce any new insights, but rather reaffirmed that intensive service probation failed to improve probation outcomes as expected.

The shortcomings of evaluation studies in corrections have been outlined by many, but are well capsulated by Rezmovic (1979) and Bennett (1979). Can some of the shortcomings in methodology account for the lack of dramatic findings, either for the total sample or for the subsample made up of male felons? Probably not. The randomization process was carefully monitored and fully executed. While the treatment intervention was clearly specified in the planning and implementation of the project, it was inadequately described in the final report (Romm, 1982). However, the lack of definition of the intervention has been corrected in the current presentation. In addition, it is clear that the implementation process was carefully documented. Probation officer contacts were precisely recorded as to number and type. Referrals were completely categorized. Follow-up periods were clearly specified and outcome measures carefully delineated.

What, then, could the problem be? It would appear that a clue is presented in the comparison of probation officer contacts between intensive service supervision and normal supervision for high risk male felons. It turns out that face-to-face contacts are higher (14 vs. 11 over a six month period) for the group under normal supervision than for the group under the intensive service plan (see Table 7). How can this be explained? There seem to be two contributing factors. First, probation officers may react with a higher level of concern when confronted with a male felon classified by an acceptable procedure as "high risk" than to a case rated as medium risk or to a misdemeanant. Since "normal" supervision for this group involves suggested contacts once or twice per month (see Figure 2), this frequency of contact is very similar to that outlined for the intensive service group. Second, within normal supervision there are three levels: high, medium and low. It seems likely that many, if not most, high risk male felons would fall into the high supervision group. Supporting this view is the fact that the high risk male felons had an average of 12.13 contacts over the first six months, much higher than for the sample as a whole (7.43), which contains a large number of misdemeanants (from Table 7).

Though intensive service was provided, those high risk male felon probationers under "normal" supervision also received a high level of service—service delivered on the basis of practical judgment and the kinds of probationers being supervised. This finding tends to blur the distinction between the two "treatments," leading to equivocal results about the efficacy of the intervention.

The other factor might well be that the *strength of treatment* was simply not sufficient to warrant the assumption that differential effects would result. This seems to be a chronic problem in correctional research and a problem inadequately dealt with in this study, despite careful planning on the part of many talented individuals and the conscientious guidance of a prestigious advisory board.

What lessons can be learned from this effort? These findings reinforce the kinds of cautions that should be raised for almost any program evaluation study, correctional or otherwise. First, we should continue to strive for experimental studies involving random assignment of subjects. As this study illustrates, such studies *can* be implemented in field settings, although compromises are often involved. Second, the treatment or treatments involved must be clearly outlined and documented. Third, implementation must be closely monitored, not only to insure the integrity of the research design but to document how the treatment delivered compares with the treatment planned. Fourth, goals, objectives and hypotheses must be clearly specified and in terms allowing for defined measurement. Fifth, especially with probation, parole and other correctional programs, the follow-up period of observation needs to be carefully defined. Within this definitional problem is the concern as to how comparisons are to be made and the length of the follow-up period. At what point are major impacts expected? In the present study, the six month outcome measure may have been too short—because the pace of justice is sometimes slow, events occurring during the fifth and sixth months might not appear in official documentation until much later, outside the measurement period.

Of greatest importance, however, is the question of how powerful an intervention has to be in order that there might be a reasonable chance that it will have an impact. Is the proposed program sufficiently different from what is currently being done to be clearly distinguishable? Can the difference be measured so that everyone is certain that something different has been accomplished? Is there preliminary evidence that program impacts are possible? Is there is a theoretic basis for expecting change?

Sometimes differences can be statistically significant but relatively small, the result of large samples being involved, with the practical value being of little importance. Let's say that the average monthly contact for a treated group is 1.7, but for the comparison group it is only 1.2 per month. While the difference may be statistically significant, is that something a probation administrator could use in developing a new program? Probably not. It may be that differences have to be very large to have even a modest impact. Thus, for example, much hope is being held out for intensive probation supervision programs that involve 15-20 face-to-face probationer contacts per month, a frequency obviously different from 2-4 such contacts. Should impact be observed in such a situation, then the refinements can be sought in further research to determine what minimal level of contacts is necessary to achieve the desired results.

In summary, the findings strongly support the concept that for a part of any probation population, even male felons, only a very minimal level of supervision is required to assure favorable outcomes. Further, the individuals for whom this low level of supervision is suitable are easily identifiable. Proper classification of these offenders requires the use of fewer probation officers in their supervision, allowing a redistribution of workload, shifting more probation officer time to those who have special problems or who present a greater potential for getting into difficulty. The improved coordination of services, however, does not seem to result in a lowering of recidivism, although it does lead to a more adequate social adjustment among participants. While there are no indications from this study as to what might affect recidivism, the increased frequency and intensity of face-to-face contacts might be an area for further exploration.

REFERENCES

Adams, Reed and Harold J. Vetter (1971). "Effectiveness of Probation Caseload Sizes: A Review of the Empirical Literature." *Criminology* 8: 333-343.

Adams, Stuart (1967). "Some Findings from Correctional Caseload Research." *Federal Probation* 31: 48-57.

Baird, Christopher (1983). *Report on Intensive Supervision Programs in Pro-*

bation and Parole. Washington, DC: U.S. National Institute of Corrections.

Banks, J., A.L. Porter, R.L. Rardin, T.R. Siler and V.E. Unger (1977). *Summary Phase I Evaluation of Intensive Special Probation Projects.* Washington, DC: U.S. National Institute of Law Enforcement and Criminal Justice.

Bennett, Lawrence (1979). "Probation, Parole and Correctional Programs - A Review of Evaluation." In *How Well Does It Work? Review of Criminal Justice Evaluation, 1978.* Washington, DC: U.S. National Institute of Law Enforcement and Criminal Justice.

Nelson, Kim, Howard Olemart and Nora Harlow (1978). *Promising Strategies in Probation and Parole.* Washington, DC: U.S. National Institute of Law Enforcement and Criminal Justice.

Petersilia, Joan, Susan Turner, James Kahan and Joyce Peterson (1985). *Granting Felons Probation: Public Risks and Alternatives.* Santa Monica, CA: Rand Corporation.

Rezmovic, Eva (1979). "Methodological Considerations in Evaluating Correctional Effectiveness: Issues and Chronic Problems." In *The Rehabilitation of Criminal Offenders: Problems and Prospects,* edited by Lee Sechrest, Susan O. White and Elizabeth D. Brown. Washington, DC: National Academy of Sciences.

Riveland, Chase and Marianne Cooke (1979). "Plan for an Experimental Project in Probation Rehabilitation." Milwaukee, WI: Wisconsin Division of Corrections working paper.

Romm, Joseph (1982). *Final Report on the National Evaluation Program— Phase II, Intensive Evaluation of Probation.* Washington, DC: System Services, Inc.

Part II

Home Confinement and Electronic Surveillance

Electronic Monitors*

by
Annesley K. Schmidt
Christine E. Curtis

Electronic monitors are new telemetry devices designed to verify that an offender is at a specified location during specified times. This technological option is stimulating a great deal of interest, in the literature, from jurisdictions considering the approach, and from manufacturers entering the market. While the concept of electronic monitoring has been discussed in the literature and small experimental efforts have been undertaken since the 1960s, the earliest of the presently operating programs only started in December 1984. The rapid development of equipment and programs has led to a number of questions. Some of these are discussed, following a description of the devices and a summary of some of the commentary in the literature about them.

INTRODUCTION

The idea of using electronic monitoring devices to track the locations of mental patients, probationers and parolees in the community was first discussed by Dr. Ralph K. Schwitzgebel in the early 1960s (1964). He then developed and tested such a device on research volunteers in Massachusetts (Schwitzgebel, 1967, 1968). Recently, technology has been

---

* *Points of view or opinions stated in this article are those of the authors and do not necessarily represent the official positions of their employers, the U.S. Department of Justice and the San Diego Association of Governments, respectively.*

Table 1

Electronic Monitoring Equipment

(Purpose: To monitor an offender's presence in a given environment where the offender is required to remain)

Devices that use a telephone at the monitored location

Continuously Signaling

A miniaturized **transmitter** is strapped to the offender and it broadcasts an encoded signal at regular intervals over a range.

A **receiver-dialer**, located in the offender's home, detects signals from the transmitter and reports to a central computer when it starts receiving the signal again: it also provides periodic checks.

A central **computer** or **receiver** accepts reports from the receiver-dialer over the telephone lines, compares them with the offender's curfew schedule, and alerts correctional officials to unauthorized absences.

Manufacturers/Distributors:

BI Home Escort. BI Incorporated, 6175 Longbow Drive, Boulder, CO 80301. Telephone 303-530-2911.

Supervisor. CONTRAC, Controlled Activities Corp., 93351 Overseas Highway, Tavernier, FL 33070. Telephone 305-852-9507.

In-House Arrest System. Correctional Services Inc., P.O. Box 2941, West Palm Beach, FL 33402. Telephone 305-683-7166.

Contac, Monitech, 419 Wakara Way, Salt Lake City, UT 84108. Telephone 801-584-2543.

Prisoner Monitoring System. Controlec, Inc., Box 48132, Niles, IL 60648. Telephone 312-966-8435.

ASC II b.* Advanced Signal Concepts, P.O. Box 1856, Clewiston, FL 33440. Telephone 813-983-2073.

Home Incarceration Unit.* Tekton I.D., Inc., 111 N. Peters, Suite 204, Norman, OK 73069. Telephone 405-360-6605.

*This device can transmit to the central unit over either telephone lines or long range wireless repeater system.

Programmed Contact

A **computer** is programmed to call the offender during the hours being monitored either randomly or at specifically selected times. It prepares reports on the results of the calls.

1) Strapped on the offender's arm is a **wristlet**, a black plastic module.

When the computer calls, the wristlet is inserted into a **verifier box** connected to the telephone to verify that the call is being answered by the offender being monitored.

Manufacturer/Distributor:

On Guard System. Digital Products Corporation, 4021 Northeast 5th Terrace, Ft. Lauderdale, FL 33334. Telephone 305-564-0521.

2) **Voice verification** technology assures that the telephone is answered by the offender being monitored.

Manufacturer/Distributor:

Provotron. VoxTron Sytems Inc., 190 Seguin St., New Braunfels, TX 78130. Telephone 512-629-4807.

*This device can transmit to the central unit over either telephone lines or long range wireless repeater system.

3) The offender wears a **wrist watch** programmed to provide a number unique to that offender at that time. The number is entered into a touch-tone telephone in response to the call.

4) **Visual verification** technology assure that the telephone is being answered by the offender being monitored.

Manufacturer/Distributor:
Luma Visual Telephone. Luma Telecom, Inc., Crystal Square 1206, 1515 Jefferson Davis Highway, Arlington, VA 22202. Telephone 703-892-4790.

Table 1 (continued)

Devices that do not use a telephone

Cellular Telephone

The **link** is a small transmitter worn by the offender.

The **locator unit,** placed in the offender's home or other approved location, receives the signal from the link, records it and relays the information by radio signals to the local area monitor.

The **local area monitor** is a microcomputer and information management system. This equipment is placed with the network manager (the leader of a small group of people who supervise the offender and encourage him to succeed). It receives information from the offender and coordinates communications among the network members. Each local network can handle 15 to 25 people.

If required, a remote management center can be added to provide increased security and back-up functions.

Manufacturer/Distributor:

SCAN System. Life Science Research Group, 515 Fargo Street, Thousand Oaks, CA 91360. Telephone 805-492-4406.

Continuously Signaling

A **transmitter** is strapped to the offender which sends out a constant signal.

A **portable receiver,** in the car of the officer who is monitoring the offender, is turned to receive the signal from the specific transmitter when the officer drives within one block of the offender's home.

Manufacturer/Distributor:

Cost-Effective Monitoring System. Dr. Walter W. McMahon, 2207 Grange Circle, Urbana, IL 61801. Telephone Day 217-333-4579 or Evening 217-367-3990.

developed by which signals are transmitted over greater distances using telephone lines or radio relays. The accompanying table provides a list of the known manufacturers. Some responded to a solicitation in the *Commerce Business Daily* for manufacturers willing to participate in the testing program at the Law Enforcement Standards Laboratory of the National Bureau of Standards (U.S. Department of Commerce, 1985). Others answered requests for bids made by jurisdictions seeking to purchase equipment. This list reflects the knowledge as of April 1986, but given the rapid rate of development additional manufacturers may have entered the field by this time.

As can be seen on the table, there are four basic technologies presently available: two use the telephone at the monitored location and two do not. Each of the technologies reflects a different approach to the problem of monitoring offenders in the community. In fact, even products within the same general technological group have important differences. These differences, and the cost and desirability of particular features, result in some of the decisions that must be made when establishing a monitoring program.

The technology is so new and the research is, thus far, so limited, that there are many questions about monitors of all kinds, on all levels. Some of these questions are: Should equipment be purchased? Can it be used legally? On whom should it be used? Will the community accept it and under what circumstances? And, will monitoring provide the community with additional protection? The U.S. National Institute of Justice, through its Fiscal Year 1986 Solicited Research Programs, suported three experimental projects that will provide answers to some of these and other important questions. Until the results of these are known, and even after, the discussions in the literature continue, and programmatic and technological questions remain.

LITERATURE ON MONITORS

The literature related to electronic surveillance focuses on three major topic areas or issues:

• Descriptions of, and justifications for, electronic surveillance and home incarceration programs.

• Legal and ethical issues, including potential abuses associated with monitoring behavior.

• Research studies documenting performance of program participants, measuring effectiveness, and assessing opinions of criminal justice personnel.

Because electronic surveillance is a relatively new field, extensive research has not been conducted to date. Most of the literature is descriptive, and addresses legal aspects of this technological approach to monitoring an offender's location.

Program Descriptions

Friel and Vaughn (1986:3) suggest that "it was not until the prison overcrowding problem created an unprecedented demand for diversion that market conditions were attractive enough to encourage the private sector to make the technology commercially available." Much of the literature discusses different types of monitoring systems starting with "Schwitzgebel's machine" (Schwitzgebel, 1969 a,b; Ingraham and Smith, 1972; Alpert and De Foor, 1984; Iverson, 1985; *Corrections Today*, 1985; Friel and Vaughn, 1985; Gable, 1986). At present the most comprehensive description of the types of technology available is provided by Daniel Ford and Annesley K. Schmidt (1985). Ralph Gable (1986) assessed developments in the electronics field, which could have future applicability to corrections, such as monitoring through cellular phones.

Schwitzgebel was the first to advocate the use of electronic monitors or telemonitoring for parolees and chronic recidivists. Others have suggested use of electronic surveillance for different types of release programs: work release, pretrial release, early release, and release on temporary passes. The monitors also have a potential use in determining the location of incarcerated inmates (Berry, 1985).Several experts warn against using electronic monitoring for offenders who would not otherwise be incarcerated, such as probationers (Schwitzgebel, 1969b; Berry, 1985; Friel and Vaughn, 1985; Gable, 1986). This might have the effect of widening the net by employing more restrictive options which may not be required to protect public safety.

The literature on home incarceration or house arrest is closely related to electronic surveillance because the two are often related programmatically. Home incarceration programs confine offenders to their homes, except for preapproved activities, with probation or community control officers personally making contacts with the individuals as well as collateral contacts with family, friends and employers (Ball and Lilly, 1983a; Corbett and Fersch, 1985; *Corrections Today*, 1985; Flynn, 1985). The justifications for home incarceration and electronic surveillance of offenders are similar. Richard Ball and Robert Lilly (1983a) cite benefits from home incarceration that may also apply to some monitoring programs:

- The stigma of sanctions, such as incarceration, is reduced.
- The offender can maintain family ties and occupational roles, which could contribute to rehabilitation.
- Home incarceration is generally less costly than construction and

maintenance of jails and prisons.

- The program protects the public by keeping the offender "off the street" while facilitating supervision.
- Home incarceration meets the public demand for punishment.

Ball and Lilly (1983b) provide some of the same arguments in support of using home incarceration for drunk drivers. They contend that mandatory sentencing laws for driving under the influence in some states have placed an excessive burden on local correctional facilities that could be minimized by the use of home incarceration. Corbett and Fersch (1985:17) also advocate house arrest, stating that "it balances the offender's right to liberty with the public right to safety and considers the cost to society of various responses to anti-social conduct."

The concepts of home incarceration and electronic monitoring have been combined in several programs to provide a less labor intensive means of supervising offenders. Several authors describe these programs, and electronic monitoring efforts have received widespread media coverage (*Corrections Magazine*, 1983; Ranii, 1983; Alpert and De Foor, 1984; *Criminal Justice Newsletter*, 1985; Flynn, 1985; Ford and Schmidt, 1985; Lilly and Wright, 1985; National Sheriff's Association, 1985; *Time Magazine*, 1985; Woolard, 1985; Brydolf, 1986; Gable, 1986; Weintraub, 1986).

The literature on electronic monitors provides additional justifications to those put forth by advocates of home incarceration. Ingraham and Smith (1972) add that electronic surveillance, by allowing the offender to work, enhances his ability to pay restitution and taxes on earnings. Schwitzgebel indicates that the technology itself has the potential to assist in the rehabilitation process. First, the device acts as a deterrent, because the offender's location is known. Second, a two-way tone communication with the parolees could provide rewards, warnings, or other signals in accordance with planned therapy. He also suggests that the gradual reduction of the level or extent of monitoring, based on performance, can enhance rehabilitation (Schwitzgebel, Schwitzgebel, Pahnke and Hurd, 1964; Gable, 1986). He states that "there is the clear danger of a tendency to use an electronic rehabilitation system merely for surveillance rather than for rehabilitation purposes" (Schwitzgebel, 1969b:607). On the negative side, some authors have warned of potential abuses of electronic surveillance. Concerns regarding this technology, which some suggest has "Orwellian" overtones, are generally associated with legal, constitutional, and ethical issues (Schwitzgebel, 1969b; Rorvik, 1974; Berry, 1985; Marx, 1985, 1986).

Legal and Ethical Issues

Del Carmen and Vaughn (1986) provide an in-depth discussion of possible infringements of consitutional rights that could be associated with electronic monitoring of offenders, including: the right to privacy, the right against self- incrimination, equal protection, search and seizure, and cruel and unusual punishment. They conclude that the constitutionality of electronic monitoring will be upheld, if challenged. Berry (1985) also raises questions regarding constitutional rights, in particular the fourth amendment, as well as concerns over societal intrusion, social and economic costs, and informed consent. These authors refer to prior U.S. Supreme Court cases on related legal issues, such as wiretapping and electronic surveillance by law enforcement, as a basis for their conclusions that monitoring may be a viable alternative to incarceration if safeguards are implemented. Several authors have recommended administrative policies and procedures, informed consent, voluntary waiver of rights, and legislation to protect offenders from abuses (*Harvard Law Review*, 1966; Schwitzgebel, 1967, 1968, 1969b; Ball and Lilly, 1984; Berry 1985; Lilly and Wright, 1985; del Carmen and Vaughn, 1986; Lilly, Ball and Lotz, 1986).

Research

In 1969, Schwitzgebel reported on a study in which 16 subjects, including an offender with over 100 arrests, voluntarily agreed to wear electronic monitors. The purpose of this research was to assess social and psychological effects of monitoring. Schwitzgebel concluded that subjects either adjusted to the monitor or rejected it within the "first several days." He suggested that this pattern is similar to recidivism among parolees, for whom the first weeks are critical to long-term adjustment (Schwitzgebel, 1969a). The presumption that some individuals will initially experience problems adjusting to monitors is an important consideration for program development.

In 1985, Lilly and Wright (1985) completed a preliminary evaluation of a home incarceration program in Kenton County, Kentucky, which utilizes electronic monitoring. (See the final chapter in this book for their latest findings.) They raised several key issues for the evaluation of electronic surveillance. However, methodological problems, including a small sample size and the lack of random assignment to experimental and control groups, limited the generalizability of their findings.

Friel and Vaughn (1986) present results of telephone interviews with probation administrators, users, and manufacturers regarding electronic monitoring of offenders. Their findings can be summarized as follows:

• Direct costs of electronic surveillance may be cheaper than construction or operational expenses of institutions, but other indirect costs, benefits, and lost opportunity costs should be considered.

• The technology may be less cost-beneficial to probation administrators than to administrators of overcrowded institutions.

• Electronic surveillance does not solve the overcrowding problem, but can be used in conjunction with other alternatives to incarceration.

• Implementation of a monitoring program in a probation department will require administrative and organizational changes (e.g., 24 hour operation, screening procedures for potential candidates).

• The technology may not be appropriate for all probation departments.

They concluded that "the ultimate empirical question is whether the technology reduces risk to the public or enhances the opportunity for rehabilitation any better than conventional supervisory strategies which cost less" (Friel and Vaughn, 1986:14).

In 1969 (b: 609), Schwitzgebel suggested that "several carefully controlled experiments could probably increase the accuracy and effectiveness" of planned implementation of electronic monitoring programs. Over 15 years later, Berry stated that there was not yet a body of empirical knowledge which assesses the utility and cost benefits of electronic surveillance (1985).

PROGRAMMATIC QUESTIONS

Monitors, at least in theory, could be used on any number of offender groups. They could be used on sentenced or unsentenced offenders. They could be used before sentencing, immediately after sentencing, or at a later point in the sentence when problems appear. They could be used to monitor house arrest, as an alternative to jail, as part of an intensive supervision program, or in the context of a work release program. All of these program possibilities have been discussed, and most of them are presently operational. However, we do not yet know if monitors are effective in these program applications, much less where they are most effective.

We also do not know which offenders should be the focus of the program. There are clearly some offenders whom nobody wants in the community. These offenders should be incarcerated. However, there are other offenders who are not so clearly dangerous and are not so obviously candidates for confinement. Can they be punished or deterred by other means? Can they be monitored in the community? Should they be monitored in the community? We do not know.

Whether particular types or groups of offenders can be monitored in a given community will depend, in part, on what that community, its judges, and its elected and political officials consider acceptable and appropriate punishment. For example, in some communities there may be strong pressure to jail drunk drivers; other communities may be satisfied if drunk drivers are required to stay home during their non-working hours with monitors used to assure that they do so. In addition to elected and appointed officials, there are other groups in the community that may feel special concerns about the establishment of a monitoring program. These might include the defense bar, MADD (Mothers Against Drunk Drivers), and the ACLU (American Civil Liberties Union). Each of these groups potentially could be strong supporters of the program if its ends were compatible with theirs, or they could be vocal adversaries. Whether or not these groups are notified before the program is started and has had the time to establish a record needs to be consciously decided.

Type of offense is clearly one factor that should be considered when determining who should be eligible for electronic monitoring. However, it is not the only factor. Should the program be limited to volunteers whose family members agree to participation by the offenders? In some instances, having the offender confined in the home could create conflicts and exert pressures on all family members. Also, are drug users, alcohol abusers, and individuals who have previously escaped from incarceration poor risks and therefore ineligible? And will employment be a requirement of participation?

Another consideration related to who can and should be monitored in the community may depend on the type of equipment selected and the structure of the program in which it is used. Some types of equipment monitor the offender continually, while other types do so only intermittently. Some devices send a signal if tampered with and some do not, so that removal of or damage to the equipment is only detected with visual inspection. And, if the equipment indicates that the offender is not where he is supposed to be or that some other problem has occurred, has the program been designed so that there will be an immediate response, or does the program staff review these indicators only on weekdays during the day? A few existing programs have the base computer located in a facility that is staffed 24 hours a day, seven days a week. They then know immediately that a problem has occurred and can send staff members to the offender's house to check and, if necessary, attempt to locate him. In other programs, the printout is reviewed in the morning and offenders are contacted to explain abnormal findings made the previous night.

Program administrators must also determine what the consequences for violations will be. Will the offender be charged with escape, lose good time credits, or be returned to a minimum, medium or maximum security facility? Next, how long *will* the offenders be monitored by the equipment? Here again the equipment is too new and the experience too limited to provide an answer. Officials at Pride, Inc., in West Palm Beach, Florida, believe that offenders can tolerate the monitors for about 90 to 120 days

(Rasmussen and Rothbart, 1986). After that, they feel, offenders begin to chafe under the restriction. And, how long *should* they be kept on the equipment? This question must be answered in the context of why the program is being operated. The answer would be quite different if the goal were retribution as opposed to merely fulfilling the requirement of the law. In Palm Beach County, it has been decided that three days on the monitor is the equivalent of one day in jail to fulfill the required mandatory sentence for a second conviction for driving while intoxicated. For other offenses the prescribed sentence is a range and, therefore, the appropriate time on the monitor is not so clear.

Can electronic monitors solve or alleviate prison and jail crowding? The answer to this question is probably "no" for a variety of reasons. First, the population selected as the target of monitoring programs may or may not otherwise be sent to jail or prison if monitors are not available. Second, the likely impact on the total crowding problem may vary widely. In a 1,000 man jail, the release of 20 monitored inmates would reduce the population by only 2 percent. In a smaller jail, more impact would be achieved by a system with a capacity for monitoring 20 inmates, the typical size of the initial purchase being made. In the prison systems of many states, with their much larger populations, more monitored inmates would have to be released before a significant reduction in population could occur. Furthermore, the cost of a monitoring program cannot be directly compared to per diem cost of incarceration. The largest component of per diem costs is staff salaries. Therefore, until the number of released inmates is large enough to affect staffing of the facility, the only savings achieved are in marginal categories such as food.

The inverse to the question about the effect of monitors on jail crowding is the question of net widening. Will offenders be sanctioned who otherwise would not be? Will offenders be more severely sanctioned? These issues deserve attention. If offenders are being monitored who would not otherwise have been incarcerated, the cost benefit equation on the use of the equipment is changed. If, on the other hand, offenders are monitored who might otherwise receive probation with little direct supervision, the question becomes, "Is the community being better protected?" At present, we do not know the answer to that question either.

Taken together, the questions of reducing prison population and net widening lead to the more basic question: Why is a monitoring program being established? Any jurisdiction establishing a program should be able to answer this. Clearly there is a wide variety of possible answers. Reduction of prison or jail population is only one. Net widening is a possibility, but is more likely an unintended by-product. Another possible answer is to better protect citizens from those offenders already in the community on some form of release. If the question cannot be answered, then the situation is equipment in search of a program, perhaps the most inappropriate way for program development to proceed.

Whatever the rationale for the monitoring program, one more issue that must be considered is the legality of the use of monitors. Thus far, there have been no known test cases. Furthermore, the question of legality obviously would differ in each jurisdiction depending on statute and appellate decisions. It would also probably differ depending on whether the monitors were being used pretrial or on sentenced offenders (see Calvello, 1985; Christensen, 1985; del Carmen and Vaughn, 1986).

Another question is: "How much will it cost?" The answer, of course, depends on the type of equipment, the number of units and whether the equipment is purchased or leased. In addition, there may be telephone charges and personnel costs. The In-House Arrest Work Release Program of the Sheriff's Stockade in Palm Beach County, Florida charges participants in the voluntary program $9.00 per day (Garcia, 1986). Within the first fourteen months of program operation, the investment in equipment had been returned by offender fees. However, if the initial amount invested is more or less, if fees are charged at a lower or higher rate, or not at all, or if the equipment is in use a greater or lesser proportion of the time, then the pay-back period will change. Some programs have incorporated a sliding scale of fees paid by offenders, based on income, to provide equal access to monitors. This can affect program revenues. Also, the pay-back period can be increased if the number of inmates or probationers eligible for monitors is insufficient to ensure that the units are in use most of the time. Program administrators should consider estimating the number of offenders meeting eligibility requirements in advance to avoid the situation faced by one California County where home detention proved to be more costly than jail partly because the number of participants was small (Contra Costa County, undated).

Additionally, there is the issue of who will pay for telephone equipment if it is required. Can an offender who otherwise would qualify for electronic monitoring be excluded because he does not have a telephone? In New Jersey, arrangements were made with the telephone company to ensure that overdue bills would be paid by the offenders so that telephone service could be reinstated, allowing their participation in the program (Goldstein, 1986).

Programs using monitors in the community function as part of the criminal justice system. Therefore, they require the cooperation of the courts and probation and parole, at a minimum. Many times, they also may involve the sheriff, other law enforcement agencies and others. As with any multi-agency effort, the lines of responsibility must be clear and the cooperation between them developed. For example, if the results of the monitoring are to be reviewed around the clock, then the base is optimally located where 24 hour staffing is already present. This facility might be a jail or a halfway house. The program, on the other hand, might be operated by the probation office. If more than one agency is involved, the division of responsibilities and expectations should be specified, preferably in writing.

A related issue is who authorizes placement in an electronic monitoring program? Should it be a judge, the local parole board, the sheriff's department, the local department of corrections, or probation staff? Conversely, which entity should be responsible for removing offenders from the program when violations occur?

Finally, what criteria will be used to assess the effectiveness of monitoring programs? A key issue is protection of the community while the offender is in the program. However, rehabilitation could also be an outcome, measured in recidivism rates, continued employment and adjustment in the community after release. The indicators of effectiveness will vary among the types of program, and should be related to the overall purpose for instituting electronic monitoring of offenders.

TECHNOLOGICAL QUESTIONS

The questions above can be viewed at a theoretical, philosophical, or program planning level. However, there are also questions or potential problems related to the functioning of the equipment itself. These questions emanate from the preliminary results of an as yet unpublished study conducted at the Law Enforcement Standards Laboratory of the U.S. National Bureau of Standards, supported by the U.S. National Institute of Justice. Information also has been gained from the experience of some of the monitoring programs. It should be noted that the comments are preliminary and often reflect testing results from what is now the *previous* generation of equipment, since the technology itself is developing so rapidly.

One problem found was telephone line incompatibility. Telephone lines carry electric current, and the characteristics of the current can vary with different telephone systems. Additionally, some telephone exchanges use very modern switching equipment and can handle pulses such as those from touch-tone phones. Others use older equipment that may have trouble handling the electronic signals transmitted by some of the monitoring systems. Whether this is a problem can only be determined specifically through a test of the local system and local exchanges and/or consultation with the local telephone company.

Another problem that appears remediable, and has been addressed by some manufacturers, is the effect of weather conditions. During windstorms and thunderstorms, both electric lines and telephone lines are whipped around and may come into contact with other lines. This may lead to arcing of the power and power surges. In the same way that most users of home computers have surge protectors placed on the incoming power lines, monitoring devices may have surge protectors placed on the incoming electrical and telephone lines. It appears that most manufacturers have installed surge protectors on their current equipment. In addition, uninterruptable power supplies are provided by some manufacturers to guarantee power to the system even during power outages.

Many devices use radio frequency signals for communication between components of the system. In some locations, radio landing beacons from airports and radio station broadcasts can interfere with the functioning of the device. Whether this is a problem is dependent on the other radio transmissions in the area where the equipment is being used and the radio frequency that the device uses.

Another potential problem is the effect of iron and steel, which may block signal transmission or create an electromagnetic field. This can occur in steel trailers or in houses where the stucco exterior is attached over a steel, chicken wire frame. Large appliances, such as refrigerators, and cast iron bathroom fixtures may also interfere with the signal. In some places, the problems often can be dealt with by moving the receiving equipment. In other settings, it may limit the offender's mobility to less than had been expected. At least one manufacturer provides repeater stations within the house to forward and amplify the signal.

These are some of the technological problems that have come to light, and many of them have already been solved. In other cases, ways to avoid them and minimize their effects have been noted. It is not surprising that they have developed, given the newness of the technologies. It would also not be surprising if additional problems come to light as broader experience with these devices is gained. It seems reasonable to assume that manufacturers will seek to solve any future problems as they have in the past.

In summary, monitors are new technological devices that offer exciting possibilities for controlling offenders in the community. However, there are still many unknowns, many issues to be considered by those establishing programs, and many questions yet to be asked and answered.

REFERENCES

Alpert, Geoffrey P. and J. Allison De Foor II (1984). "Florida's Invisible Jails." *Judges Journal* 23 (Fall):33, 46.

Ball, Richard A. and J. Robert Lilly (1983a). "Home Incarceration: An Alternative to Total Incarceration." Presented at the IX International Meeting of the Society of Criminology, Vienna, Austria.

———(1983b). "The Potential Use of Home Incarceration with Drunken Drivers." Paper presented at the American Society of Criminology Meeting, Denver.

———(1986). "A Theoretical Examination of Home Incarceration." *Federal Probation* (March):17-24.

Berry, Bonnie (1985). "Electronic Jails: A New Criminal Justice Concern." *Justice Quarterly* 2:1 (March).

Brydolf, Libby (1986). "High-Tech to Cut Costs of Justice." *San Diego Transcript* (February 5):1a, 6a.

Calvello, Anthony (1985). "Electronic Monitors." Memorandum to Richard L. Jordan by Public Defender, Palm Beach County, FL (October 2).

Christensen, Charlie (Assistant Attorney General) (1985). "Informal Opinion No. 83-81." Letter to William C. Vickery, Director, Division of Corrections, State of Utah (April 24).

Contra Costa County, Adult Probation Department (undated). "Adult Home Detention Program, End of Project Report, December 1983 through April 1985." Photocopy.

Corbett, Ronald and Elsworth Fersch (1985). "Home as Prison: Use of House Arrest." *Federal Probation* L(March):13-17.

Corrections Magazine (1983). "Probation and Bracelets: The Spiderman Solution" IX:3 (June):4.

Corrections Today (1985). "Florida's Offenders Under House Arrest" (October):105.

Criminal Justice Newsletter (1985). "Electronic Monitoring of Probationers on the Increase" 16:20 (October 15):4-6.

del Carmen, Rolando, V. and Joseph B. Vaughn (1986). "Legal Issues in the Use of Electronic Surveillance in Probation." *Federal Probation* L(June):60-69.

Flynn, Leonard (1985). "Community Control 'House Arrest'...A Cooperative Effort Effectively Implemented." *APPA Perspectives* 9:3 (Summer):1-4.

Ford, Daniel and Annesley K. Schmidt (1985). "Electronically Monitored Home Confinement." *NIJ Reports.* 194 (November):2-6.

Friel, Charles M. and Joseph B. Vaughn (1986). "A Consumer's Guide to the Electronic Surveillance of Probationers." *Federal Probation* L(September).

Gable (formerly Schwitzgebel), Ralph K. (1986). "Applications of Personal Telemonitoring to Current Problems in Corrections." *Journal of Criminal Justice* 14:167-175.

Garcia, Eugene D. (1986). "In-House Arrest Work Release Program." Photocopy and personal communication (February 15).

Goldstein, Harvey (1986). Personal communication (March).

Harvard Law Review (1966). "Anthropotelemetry: Dr. Schwitzgebel's Machine" 80:403-421.

Ingraham, Barton L. and Gerald Smith (1972). "Use of Electronics in Observation and Control of Human Behavior." *Issues in Criminology* 7(2):35-53.

Iverson, Wesley R. (1985). "High-Tech Leg Irons Put to the Test." *Electronics Week* (March 4):30.

Lilly, J. Robert and Jennifer Wright (1985). "Home Incarceration with Electronic Monitoring in Kenton County, Kentucky: A Preliminary Report." Submitted to the Kentucky Department of Corrections (December).

Liliy, J. Robert, Richard A. Ball and W. Robert Lotz, Jr. (1986). "Electronic Jail Revisited." *Justice Quarterly* 3:3 (September):353-361.

Marx, Gary T. (1985). "The New Surveillance." *Technology Review* 45 (May-June):43-48.

——(1986). "I'll Be Watching You." *Dissent* (Winter):26-34.

National Bureau of Standards (forthcoming). *Testing of Electronic Monitoring Devices.*

National Sheriff's Association (1985). "Electronic Prison Less Costly." *Sheriff's Roll Call* II(2):8.

Ranii, D. (1983). "Ankle Signal Linked to Computer May Monitor Probationers in New Mexico." *National Law Journal* (March 28):3, 38.

Rasmussen, Fred and Glen Rothbart (1986). Personal communication (April).

Rorvik, D. (1974). "Behavior Control: Big Brother Comes." *Intellectual Digest* (January):17-20.

Schwitzgebel (now Gable), Ralph K. (1967). "Electronic Innovation in Behavioral Sciences: A Call to Responsibility." *American Psychologist* 22:364-370.

——(1968). "Electronic Alternatives to Imprisonment." *Lex et Scientia* 5:3 (July-Sept.):99-104.

——(1969a). "Development of an Electronic Rehabilitation System for Parolees." *Law and Computer Technology* 2(March):9-12.

——(1969b). "Issues in the Use of an Electronic Rehabilitation System with Chronic Recidivists." *Law and Society Review* III(4):597-611.

Schwitzgebel (now Gable), Ralph, Robert Schwitzgebel (now Gebel), Walter N. Pahnke and William Sprech Hurd (1964). "A Program of Research in Behavior Electronics." *Behavioral Science* 9:233-238.

Time Magazine (1985). "Spiderman's Net: An Electronic Alternative to Prison" (October 14):93.

U.S. Department of Commerce (1985). "Electronic Monitoring Devices." *Commerce Business Daily* (February 11):21.

Weintraub, Daniel M. (1986). "Some Convicts Will Serve Their Sentences at Home." *Los Angeles Times* (February 5).

Woolard, Andrea (1985). "Comic Strip Inspires Electronic Surveillance Device for Parolees." *Engineering Times* 7:5 (May):16-17.

Planning for Change: The Use of Electronic Monitoring as a Correctional Alternative

by
Joseph B. Vaughn

In January 1985 the Texas Criminal Justice Policy Council formed a study committee to examine the feasibility of using house arrest and electronic monitoring as a correctional alternative. The research effort focused on the existing technology, current programs, legal issues, philosophic and policy concerns, and development of program applications. Although the technology may be a useful tool in the repertoire of the criminal justice system, it is not the sole remedy for the overcrowding problem and cannot serve as a substitute for sound correctional policy making.

INTRODUCTION

Not unlike other states, Texas is experiencing a continuing problem of prison overcrowding. Between 1974 and 1983 there was a 142 percent increase in new admissions to the state's prison system. Assuming no

153

changes in current policies, new admissions are expected to rise by another 17.6 percent between 1985 and 1991 (Texas Criminal Justice Policy Council, 1986). In addition to the exponential increase in the number of new admissions to prison, the Texas system is under a federal court order which requires substantial and costly facility and program improvements (Ruiz v. Estelle, 1980). This situation is not unique to Texas, however. Most states, territories, and the District of Columbia are under court orders to reduce prison overcrowding or to remedy other confinement conditions (Reid, 1985).

Institutional overcrowding in the United States has reached crisis proportions. Simultaneously, practitioners, policymakers and the public have begun to question the very foundations of criminal justice policy in an attempt to balance the relative merits of rehabilitation, deterrence, punishment, public safety, and the utilization of ever-decreasing fiscal resources in the most cost-effective manner.

Recognizing that effective change must be accomplished through a systemic approach, in 1983 Texas created the Criminal Justice Policy Council, whose membership includes the governor, lieutenant governor, speaker of the house of representatives, secretary of state, two state representatives, a county sheriff, district attorney, and a representative from a state university. The council's primary objective is to conduct an in-depth analysis of the criminal justice system and develop a coherent policy addressing the critical problems of the system.

A number of correctional alternatives have been proposed to stem the growing incarceration rates, most recently the use of house arrest and electronic monitoring to supervise offenders in the community. In December 1985, the Criminal Justice Policy Council endorsed a motion to identify potential applications of the technology in Texas. The council's Electronic Monitoring and House Arrest Study Committee includes representatives from the state correctional agencies, county sheriffs and state university.

The systemic nature of the criminal justice system requires that any initiative toward problem resolution be coordinated among the affected agencies and policymakers. The policy council, in conjunction with the study committee, provided a vehicle to achieve that coordination. Because formalized use of the technology is still in its infancy, the primary approach of the committee was to study its utility from a macro-perspective. The study focused on several basic areas: the existing technology, current programs, legal issues, philosophic and policy concerns, and development of program applications. While the information was generated for application in Texas, the basic issues examined and the planning process are generalizable to other agencies that must plan for changes associated with adoption of the technology.

EXISTING TECHNOLOGY

One of the earliest references to the use of an electronic monitoring device was recorded in the literature over 20 years ago, when the development of a portable device for tracking the location of individuals was announced. The system was utilized from 1964 through 1970 to monitor the location of parolees, mental patients, and research volunteers in Massachusetts (Gable, 1986).

Advances in technology and favorable marketing conditions created by overcrowding and fiscal constraints have led to a recent rediscovery of the possible applications of telemetry as a correctional alternative. One of the first formalized uses of the technology by a criminal justice agency occurred during 1983 in Albuquerque, New Mexico. District Court Judge Jack Love was inspired by a "Spiderman" comic strip to experiment with the concept of enforcing house arrest with the aid of an electronic monitoring device (Niederberger, 1984). Subsequent to that experiment, programs were implemented in Florida. The initial evaluations of those programs were favorable, prompting adoption of the concept in various locations.

Functional Characteristics

Current systems can be placed in two broad categories: those requiring a telephone to operate, and those which do not. The most prevalent systems are those using telephone lines to communicate between the offender's home and a central office. The first type of these systems, referred to in the earliest literature as "active" systems, consists of a transmitter, a receiver-dialer unit, and a central office computer or receiver unit. A transmitter is strapped to the offender and broadcasts an encoded signal to the receiver located in the offender's home. The receiver is connected by the telephone to the central office computer or receiver unit. When the transmitter being worn by the offender is within range of the home receiver, the system indicates that he is at the residence. When the offender goes beyond the range of the receiver unit the signal from the transmitter is not received and the system indicates absence. If the offender leaves home during an unauthorized period, a violation report is generated. If, however, the offender is away from home during an authorized period, the times of arrival and departure are noted but no violation report is generated.

A second type of unit utilizing the telephone lines for communication has been referred to in the earlier literature as a "passive" system. It consists of a central office computer, an encoder device, and a verifier box. The encoder device is worn either on the wrist or ankle by the offender. The computer is programmed to generate either random calls or to call at specific times to the offender's home. The offender is required to provide voice identification and then insert the encoder device into the verifier box, confirming his identity. The system will provide exception reports if the phone is not answered, if a busy signal is received, or if the offender fails to properly insert the encoder device into the verifier box.

Currently under development is a passive system which relies on computerized voice identification. The offender, who is not required to wear any type of device, must answer a series of random questions which are then matched by the computer with a previously supplied exemplar of his voice.

The essential difference between the active and passive systems is that the active system operates continuously, monitoring the time the offender arrives and departs. The passive system verifies the presence of the offender only at the time the telephone call is made from the central office. The term "passive" is somewhat misleading in that the offender is required to perform certain functions.

The second major category of systems includes those devices that do not rely on telecommunications equipment. One such device consists of a transmitter that emits a radio signal, and a portable receiver. The receiver is placed in the monitoring official's car and receives the signal from the transmitter when it is within one block of the offender. Periodic checks of residential areas are made during the time period the offenders are required to be home. The device may also be used to make random checks at places of employment, treatment centers, or other locations to confirm the presence of the offender.

Although none are known to be in use, the technology exists to operate a system similar to those relying on telecommunications by radio transmitters. Under such a system the offender wears a personal transmitter which sends a signal to the home receiver. The receiver records the information and then sends it by radio signal to a central location.

During the council's study, ten vendors of such equipment were interviewed. Except for field testing, four of the companies did not yet have their equipment functioning in a criminal justice agency program. One of those manufacturers was in the process of developing a prototype of the equipment, and another was awaiting final approval from the Federal Communications Commission.

While these newer systems are similar, there are differences in the functional characteristics that should be considered by an agency prior to purchase. Most of the systems require the offender to wear a transmitter either around his ankle, waist, wrist, or neck. Where the transmitter is worn has no known effect on the reliability of the equipment, but it may raise other issues. If the device is not concealable under normal clothing the person may suffer unnecessary stigmatization. In addition, certain occupations may prohibit the wearing of jewelry or other items around the wrist or neck for safety reasons. Because the devices are relatively new, it is not yet possible to assess their durability. Transmitters worn on one part of the body may be subject to more abuse than those worn elsewhere. Some manufacturers offer equipment that may be worn by the person in one of several places. Such systems will allow an agency more flexibility in meeting the needs of individual offenders.

Tamper-proof transmitters are available from five of the manufacturers. The option detects attempts to remove the device and reports it to the central computer. While a tamper-proof transmitter is a security benefit, it may also increase the costs. Whether or not the option is cost beneficial is open to debate. If the probationer takes the transmitter off and leaves it next to the telephone while going out for a night on the town, the system is clearly jeopardized. With a tamper-proof capability any attempt to do so would be detected. If, however, the person wishes to abscond and removes the device while he is away from home during an authorized time, his absence would not be discovered until he violated his curfew by failing to return home. In order for the receiver to record attempts to tamper with the transmitter, the tampering must occur while the transmitter is within range of the receiver.

Without the tamper-proof option, removal might not be discovered until the device was visually inspected. However, those units that do not detect tampering are secured with a special band that cannot be removed without being destroyed (and the bands are not commercially available to individuals). The benefit of tamper-proofing, therefore, may only be the psychological effect on the offender.

In some areas more than others, the source of electricity used to energize the system may create difficulties. A power outage may cause the computer to crash, eliminating its capacity to monitor offenders and causing a loss of data in open files. A power failure at the offender's home will result in the monitor ceasing to function. In some systems this will generate a false violation report. Battery backup power suppplies for both the computer and the monitoring unit in the home are desirable features, particularly in areas subject to frequent power outages. If the batteries in the transmitter fail, no signal will be sent to the receiver and the computer may register a curfew violation. Some products have switching devices which allow the agency to turn off the battery while the unit is not being used, increasing the unit's shelf life. Others have a feedback mechanism in the system indicating when the batteries are beginning to run down and need to be replaced. That option should eliminate false violation reports caused by battery failures.

Since most of the equipment available requires the use of a telephone, the quality of local telephone service may affect the system's reliability. If the manufacturer's minimum requirements and the quality of phone lines are a poor match, the technology may be a poor investment.

Finally, one should realize that the offender must have a home, and in most instances a phone, to qualify for the program. While this seems obvious, the requirement may play havoc with the potential cost benefits to be realized from the technology. Individuals who would otherwise be incarcerated may not qualify since their indigency prevents them from finding an appropriate residence or paying for telephone installation and service. While it is easy to dismiss this problem with the dictum "no home, no phone, no program," the circumstance of indigency may work against the cost benefits to be achieved with the technology. This raises the issue of whether the department should absorb the cost of telephone installation and service in deserving cases. Obviously, there is a point of diminishing returns in how much the offender can contribute to the operation of the system and how far the agency can go in underwriting the offender.

Cost Benefits

Estimated average daily costs for acquisition of the equipment range from $1.29 to $9.04 for outright purchase, from $0.95 to $7.00 for lease-purchase agreements, and from $1.91 to $7.00 for straight lease agreements.

It is premature to attempt to determine the actual cost benefits of the technology. Only recently has it been introduced to the field, and only time will tell whether the benefits derived outweigh the costs. The question of cost benefit is complex, and assessments vary depending upon point of view, such as the sheriff with an overcrowded jail versus the probation department that may have to pay for the technology. In addition to the direct cost of purchasing equipment, there are the indirect costs encountered in operating the system. Consideration also must be given to lost opportunity costs and benefits (what other programs could have been initiated or expanded with the funds used to purchase the surveillance equipment?), as well as nonmonetary costs and benefits.

Probably the primary selling point of the technology is its potential cost savings compared to the cost of operating institutions and new construction. The institutional overcrowding problem has made policymakers keenly aware of the extraordinary costs associated with incarceration. Institutional operating costs vary but a recent study suggests they may well range between $15 and $50 per inmate per day. Similarly, the cost of new construction varies from $25,000 to $75,000 or more per bed depending upon the level of architectural security (Funke, 1985). In Texas, daily institutional operating costs are estimated to range from $40 to $56 per inmate, depending upon the particular agency and type of supervision afforded.

From this perspective, there is no question that the direct cost of electronically supervising offenders in the community is cheaper than incarceration. In some instances, however, costs for monitoring may exceed current costs of minimal supervision by probation officials. Although costs vary among manufacturers and as a function of the number of units acquired, the current direct cost of a system ranges from $.95 to $9.04 per day. This may represent an attractive cost trade-off for policymakers who can see savings not only in institutional operating costs, but in the reduced need for future construction.

From the agency administrator's point of view, the technology may not be cost beneficial. Relatively speaking, public expenditures for the administration of justice are a zero-sum game. Funds expended for one purpose are no longer available for another. Administrators need to properly assess the priority to be attached to the acquisition of the technology relative to other departmental needs.

In a survey of 23 probation administrators throughout the United States considered to be informed on the topic, most agreed that the technology should only be used to divert offenders who would be otherwise incarcerated. If the technology is simply used with individuals who would be granted probation or parole anyway, there is no cost savings relative to institutional costs. Unless it can be demonstrated that use of the technology with typical offenders reduces recidivism more than conventional supervisory strategies, there would be no savings from a public safety perspective. It is likely that if the technology is used only to enhance surveillance of people who should be granted probation or parole in the first instance, the result will be a widening of the correctional net, increasing costs with no noticeable benefit (Friel and Vaughn, 1986).

There are a variety of potential monetary benefits which could flow from the use of the technology. Obviously money saved by diverting offenders can well be used in other ways. However, the nonmonetary humanistic benefits that might be derived from the technology are equally attractive. For example, the secondary effects of incarceration are neither few nor trivial. Pretrial detainees, for instance, who are unable to make bond or be released on their own recognizance may lose their jobs, and/or residence, default on their car payments, and lose their ability to support their families. In this case policymakers must weigh the secondary effects of incarceration against the magnitude of the risk to public safety and failure-to-appear rate. Although the actual calculation of such tradeoffs is complex, the cost/benefit issue is simple: it is neither humanistically nor economically beneficial to hold people in prison or jail who do not need to be there (Nagel, Wice and Neef, 1977).

Advocates of electronic monitoring argue that the technology has the potential to reduce jail and prison populations. If successful, depending upon local conditions, monitoring could (1) reduce the rate of capital expansion in the future; (2) obviate the need for new construction; or (3) reduce the population in existing facilities. Critics of the technology express skepticism about the third alleged benefit. They suggest that even if offenders were diverted from existing institutions, thereby making bed space available, the beds would be filled anyway. The result would not be a reduction in operating costs; on the contrary, it would simply increase overall public expenditures by the cost associated with the purchase of the technology (Conrad and Rector, 1977).

If the proposed benefits are to be realized by the correctional community and the public, then the cost of the technology must be reasonable, the equipment reliable, operation efficient, training requirements minimal, and noticeable enhancements in public safety achieved. Prudent public policy requires that the private sector absorb the research and development costs prior to offering the technology to the correctional community. This suggests that an agency administrator should look not only at the comparative cost among the different systems currently in the marketplace, but also assess the extent and quality of the research and development that stand behind the products. Purchase of an unreliable system requiring a high degree of maintenance may prove to be an irrevocable mistake, resulting in professional embarrassment and loss of public confidence.

CURRENT USE OF THE TECHNOLOGY

Of the ten programs examined by the Electronic Monitoring and House Arrest Study Committee (Vaughn, 1986), four were operated on the state level and six at the county level. These include: Department of Corrections and Rehabilitation, Dade County, FL; Sheriff's Department, Palm Beach, FL; Pride, Incorporated, West Palm Beach, FL; Department of Probation and Parole, Kenton County, KY; Michigan Department of Corrections; New Jersey Administrative Office of the Courts, Intensive Supervision Program; Oklahoma Department of Corrections; Clackamas County Community Corrections, Oregon City, OR; Linn County In-House Arrest Program, Albany, OR; and the Utah State Department of Corrections.

New Jersey uses electronic monitoring only as a component of its Intensive Supervision Program (ISP). Oklahoma and Michigan have little or no experience in the actual monitoring of offenders, while Utah has experienced equipment and programmatic difficulties that have hampered implementation. The Palm Beach County Sheriff's Department, and Pride, Incorporated (a private concern which provides probation supervision on a contract basis), have the longest running programs of those examined.

The type of offender eligible for the different programs varies from agency to agency. As might be expected, the states have developed applications directed toward felony offenders, either as a diversionary measure, or to supplement ISP programs. Only two of the counties use the technology on felony offenders, and in one of those counties only for the least serious felonies. With funding obtained from the National Highway

Table 1

Electronic Monitoring Programs

Agency	Date Began	Current Application	Average Length of Monitoring	Number Currently Monitored	Number Completed Program	Number Failed Program	Failure Rate
State of Utah	Apr 85	ISP Probation & Parole	2 Mos.	14	n/a	Several	n/a
State of Oklahoma	Not Begun	Diversion for felons in state prison	n/a	n/a	n/a	n/a	n/a
State of Michigan	Apr 85	Prison diversion for recidivist felony property offenders	n/a	n/a	n/a	n/a	n/a
Dade Co. Florida	Jul 85	County jail work furlough/Pre-trial release	40-60 Days	10	9	1	.10
Kenton Co. Kentucky	May 85	Jail diversion— Misd./Class D felony	30 Days	4	31	3	.096
Linn Co. Oregon	Oct 85	Jail diversion— primarily DUI	30 Days	15	29	3	.10
*State of New Jersey	Jun 83	Complement to ISP prison releasees	n/a	364 ISP	Approx. 130 ISP	n/a	Approx. 20% ISP
Palm Beach Co., Fla.	Dec 84	County jail work release	60 Days	20	116	3	.025
Clackamas Co., Or.	Apr 85	Jail diversion— misd. & felons Pre-trial release	30 Days	16	75	2	.026
Pride, Inc. West Palm Beach, Fla.	Dec 84	Misdemeanant jail diversion	4 Mos.	16	110	3	.027

*Note: New Jersey figures reflect all offenders under ISP, not only those under electronic monitoring.

Safety Commission, Linn County, Oregon primarily uses electronic monitoring to divert persons convicted of driving under the influence of intoxicants from the county jail.

Offenders are placed under electronic supervision for varying periods of time, generally ranging from one to four months. Most of the programs have a limited number of persons being monitored at any one time, ranging from four to 20 individuals.

While the amount of experience is extremely limited, the failure rate (failure to comply with program restrictions) is low: 10 percent or less. Excluding the figures for New Jersey, which cover all persons under ISP and are not restricted to those under electronic supervision, 370 people had completed the programs at the time of the study, with an overall failure rate of four percent. It is important to note, however, that these figures represent only the county programs, which typically have lower risk offenders than the state programs.

In keeping with the existing technology and prior experience of other agencies, potential applications for electronic monitoring and house arrest were developed by the study committee for use in Texas by the Commission on Jail Standards, the Juvenile Probation Commission, the Youth Commission, the Adult Probation Commission, and the Board of Pardons and Paroles. The programs are directed toward increasing the efficiency of agency officials, diversion of offenders from institutions or more restrictive forms of supervision, and a reduction in costs and institutional overcrowding. It is estimated that the programs may address an eligible population of 4,900 offenders.

A preliminary analysis of the data supplied by the vendors and agency representatives indicates the technology offers the potential for a reduction of corrections costs. Estimates of cost reduction for an individual offender range from $18.96 to $46.96 per day for some programs. Other programs may experience an increased cost of $2.04 to $9.04 per day. The divergence in projected costs results from several factors: the variety of funding schemes available for purchase or lease of equipment, the number and type of offenders placed in a program, and the current cost to an agency for supervision or incarceration. For example, the state's cost for supervision of a probationer, depending on the type of program utilized, ranges from $.40 to $28.00 per day, while equipment costs for electronic monitoring programs range from $.95 to $9.04 per day. However, these projections are tenuous at best. It would be less than prudent, given the limited amount of knowledge available, to make policy decisions solely on these projections. A possibility exists that personnel costs, administrative overhead, the actual failure rate of offenders in the programs, and unanticipated outside influences, may negate any hoped-for reduction in base expenditures. Aside from cost, there are other concerns that must be addressed if sound correctional policy is to be formulated.

ADMINISTRATIVE CONCERNS

By its very nature, electronic monitoring is a 24 hour per day service. Prior to implementing a system, the department must carefully specify the procedures to be followed in the event a curfew violation is reported. Several alternatives are possible. The monitors can simply call the offender on the phone to determine whether it is a false report. However, positive identification by voice is a problem. Another alternative is for the monitor to record the alleged violation and forward the report to the supervising officer, who would confront the individual the next day. A third alternative is for the monitor to call an officer who would then proceed to the person's residence to determine whether it is a false report. Obviously this is more costly, and raises the prospect of potential personnel problems.

Criminal justice employees may argue that they are too highly paid and skilled to be spending their evening hours and weekends checking curfew violations reported by a computer. While this may be a valid criticism, it could also be argued that the technology provides an opportunity to free the officer to do what he does best. The department could hire surveillance officers who need not be as highly paid or well trained as probation or parole officers since their sole function would be to follow up reported curfew violations.

Depending upon the number of offenders under surveillance, one surveillance officer could be assigned to each caseload, or possibly to two or three caseloads. The actual number of officers needed would depend upon the number of offenders in the system and the number of violations reported. If a large number of violations were reported, then a larger number of surveillance officer would appear to be required. However, it might be that the wrong kind of offender is being put under surveillance in the first place, or the equipment is unreliable and producing a large number of false alarms. If screening procedures are effective and the equipment is reliable, the number of reported violations should be low.

It is recommended that agencies design operating procedures and training programs prior to implementing the system. It would be counterproductive to purchase a system, place probationers under surveillance and then, as experience is gained, determine what procedures and training would have been appropriate. One of the first priorities should be the screening criteria to be used in determining appropriate candidates. Different procedures may have to be established, depending upon whether the potential candidates will be pretrial or posttrial, juveniles or adults.

The offender will require some training in the technology. A short orientation program should be instituted to explain the purpose of the technology, how it works, care and maintenance of the equipment, what to do if the equipment fails, and the department's policy in the event of a curfew violation.

Monitors will have to be hired and trained to operate the equipment. Procedures to be considered include how to enter, update, modify, and expunge information in the computer, and what to do in the case of reported violations. An important training consideration is what to do if the system crashes, as in the case of a power outage or mechanical failure. Depending on the manufacturer, the monitor may have to be trained in backing up and recovering the information contained in the system in order to protect the data against a system failure.

An important consideration is system security. It is a general principle of computer security to administratively separate computer operators from those authorized to make changes in the system. It is recommended that one individual, possibly the supervisor of the electronic monitoring program, be empowered to authorize changes, but be prevented from having physical access to the hardware. All the changes would be made by the computer operator, and the system should produce a daily log of all changes and modifications. It would be the supervisor's responsibility to verify whether the changes made correspond with those which were authorized. This check and balance should protect the system from inadvertent as well as unauthorized changes.

Finally, the department will need to develop procedures for officers to follow in the event of a reported curfew violation. Certainly, discretion must be exercised, since the report could result from mechanical error rather than an actual curfew violation. As with conventional probation, a curfew violation should not necessarily result in a revocation.

Should a department interested in electronic monitoring consider entering into a contract for the monitoring service? It is quite conceivable, for example, for private investors to purchase electronic surveillance systems and offer to provide contractual monitoring services. This could be cost beneficial since the department would not have to make a capital investment in the equipment, nor be concerned with maintenance, or with hiring, training, or supervising the monitors.

The department should determine whether the contractor has a proprietary interest in the particular hardware system being used. Those contractors with a proprietary interest in the hardware may well be willing to live with an undependable system, rather than change systems, as long as the department is willing to pay for the service. This would be unwise, particularly if the unreliability of the system reduced its integrity in the eyes of both agency employees and offenders. In addition, an unreliable system may jeopardize public safety.

PHILOSOPHIC CONCERNS

Interviews with probation administrators (Friel and Vaughn, 1986) suggest there is a wide range of philosophic attitudes toward the technology. On the one hand, some see it as a useful tool that could find a proper place in probation. Others see it as one step beyond what probation is supposed to be. Most administrators, however, expressed a philosophic ambivalence about the technology. They realize that probation must change with the times, but are uncertain whether electronic monitoring is an appropriate change of direction for probation. While mildly interested in the technology, they would rather let some other agency experiment with its use before taking the plunge themselves.

It may be that the differences found among the administrators' attitudes emanate from divergent views as to the purpose of probation. Some see probation as primarily a surveillance function, and although they are not opposed to rehabilitation, they are unlikely to take risks when asked to choose between these two objectives. In all likelihood, administrators who hold this view will come more readily to the use of electronic monitoring.

Other administrators approach probation from a more humanistic perspective. While they do not discount their responsibility to assure public safety, they give relatively more emphasis to the rehabilitative goals of probation. These administrators might argue that the purpose of probation is to allow offenders to demonstrate that they can be law abiding citizens. While some degree of surveillance is prudent, the probationer must be given enough room to demonstrate trustworthiness. From this point of view, some administrators feel that electronic monitoring demonstrates distrust, and therefore exceeds the proper scope of probation.

POTENTIAL ABUSES OF THE TECHNOLOGY

Electronic monitoring can be a useful tool in the repertoire of criminal justice strategies. By the same token, it can be abused.

The primary use of the technology should be the diversion of individuals who would otherwise be sentenced to prison or jail. Even allowing for the conservative nature of decision making in criminal justice, many of those currently incarcerated need the added surveillance that an institution provides. Thus, diversion of these individuals will require more extensive surveillance in the community. Other things being equal, the use of electronic monitoring in this circumstance seems appropriate. Using the technology with individuals who would be granted release anyway is impractical, since it is likely to raise costs without necessarily increasing benefits. In addition, it could needlessly widen the correctional net and be an undue invasion of privacy. It is not inconceivable that judges and prosecutors enamored of the technology could adopt the policy of including everyone under community supervision in an electronic monitoring program. This excessive use of the technology should be avoided.

Being diverted from prison or jail is a benefit to the offender, but excessively long periods of house arrest may have adverse effects. Some might argue, for instance, that it would be cost beneficial to use electronic monitoring to hold people under house arrest for 24 hours a day. If this condition were imposed for any length of time it would be abusive in two ways. First, if the offender represented such a threat to the community that prolonged house arrest was necessary, that individual needs to be in an institution. Second, such protracted and continuous confinement is contrary to the purposes of diversion.

To a lesser extent, and for the same reasons, long-term partial confinement during weekday evenings and weekends can be abusive. Such a regimen of confinement may be reasonable for several months, but if an individual has demonstrated that he can work during the day and obey curfew restrictions in the evening and on weekends, why continue such extensive monitoring? Would it not be better to reduce the level of surveillance and use the equipment on some other probationer in need of more extensive supervision?

While one should never rule out the possibility of litigation, if the technology is used appropriately litigation is unlikely. Since offenders diverted to the program would have been incarcerated otherwise, they are not likely to sue because prison is a less desirable alternative (del Carmen and Vaughn, 1986). In fact, electronic monitoring is a "bird nest on the ground" for a defense attorney looking for leverage in plea negotiation, and therein lies a potential abuse. The busy prosecutor may become too willing to negotiate pleas resulting in use of electronic monitoring, when the more appropriate alternative from the perspective of public safety would be incarceration. For this reason it is critical to involve both the prosecutor and the courts in developing diversionary policy long before the purchase of a system.

The technology should not be conceived as a quick fix for the complicated problem of overcrowded jails and prisons. A community or state facing overcrowding problems needs to conduct an in-depth analysis of why the problem exists, and identify various alternatives to ameliorate the situation. Electronic monitoring might be a useful tool, but certainly is not a substitute for sound correctional policy development.

Although practical experience is limited, common sense suggests that certain kinds of offenders may be inappropriate candidates for electronic monitoring programs. Given the current public sensitivity towards the treatment of sexual offenders, it may not be wise to include them in the program at first. This is not to say that such individuals could not benefit from the program, but that subsequent violations committed by sexual offenders under electronic surveillance may arouse such a strong community reaction that it might jeopardize the use of the technology with other suitable offenders. Common sense also suggests that offenders with a history of spouse or child abuse are not suitable candidates. In this case, the use of the technology could place family members in danger if they were residing with the offender.

Finally, one needs to carefully consider the potential use of the technology with juveniles. Communities vary, both in the extent of delinquency and their corresponding tolerance for the criminalization of the juvenile justice system, but electronic monitoring could be a very effective means of responding to early signs of delinquency. There is a danger, though, that the juvenile justice net might be widened too far; the ill effects of labeling might result from such an overreaction to deviance.

CONCLUSION

It is premature to attempt to determine the actual cost benefits of an electronic monitoring program. The technology has been only recently introduced to the correctional field and time must pass before one can determine if the benefits outweigh the costs. One must also consider the lost opportunity costs: other programs that could have been initiated or expanded with the funds used to purchase the surveillance equipment.

The nonmonetary benefits to be realized from use of the technology are as important as fiscal concerns. Policymakers must weigh the effects of incarceration of the individual against the magnitude of risk to public safety. It is neither humanistically nor economically beneficial to incarcerate people who are capable of functioning under community supervision.

Advocates of electronic monitoring argue that the technology has the potential to reduce jail and prison populations. Whether or not this will occur is as yet unknown. The technology may be a useful tool for reduction of overcrowding, but it is not the sole answer to the problem; it cannot serve as a substitute for sound correctional planning.

While it would be premature to make any assumptions based upon the limited data available, the relatively low failure rate of offenders under electronic supervision is encouraging, particularly when contrasted with the higher rate of failure experienced by the ISP program, which has used the technology only on a very limited basis. It may well be that electronic monitoring is best suited for use with low risk offenders. Additional research is needed to confirm or refute the preliminary indications.

There are many factors to consider prior to implementation of an electronic monitoring program, including why one wants to use electronic supervision, and how the program will be implemented? The technology has the potential to become a useful tool for the correctional administrator, but should not be used if other supervision techniques, which are less expensive or less intrusive, will work equally well.

REFERENCES

Conrad, J.P. and M.G. Rector (1977). *Should We Build More Prisons?* Hackensack, NJ: National Council on Crime and Delinquency.

del Carmen, R.V. and J.B. Vaughn (1986). "Legal Issues in the Use of Electronic Monitoring in Probation." *Federal Probation Quarterly* L(2):60-69 (June).

Friel, C.M. and J.B. Vaughn (1986). "A Consumer's Guide to the Electronic Surveillance of Probationers." *Federal Probation Quarterly* L(3):3-14 (September).

Funke, G.S. (1985) "Economics of Prison Crowding." *Annals of the American Academy of Political and Social Science* 478 (March): 86-99

Gable, R.K. (1986)."Application of Personal Telemonitoring to Current Problems in Corrections." *Journal of Criminal Justice* 14:167-176

Nagel, S., P. Wice and M. Neef (1977). *Too Much or Too Little Police: The Example of Pretrial Release*. Beverly Hills, CA: Sage.

Niederberger, W. (1984). "Can Science Save Us Revisited." Paper presented at the annual meeting of the American Society of Criminology, Cincinnati, OH

Reid, S.T. (1985). *Crime and Criminology,* Fourth edition. New York: Holt, Rinehart and Winston.

Ruiz v. Estelle, 503 F. Supp. 1265 (S.D. Texas 1980), affirmed in part, 679 F. 2d 1115 (5th Circuit 1983).

Texas Criminal Justice Policy Council (1986). *Electronic Monitoring and House Arrest Test Project*. Grant application submitted to the U.S. National Institute of Justice.

Vaughn, J.B. (1986). *Electronic Monitoring of Offenders*. Austin: Texas Criminal Justice Policy Council.

Home Confinement and Electronic Surveillance

by
Thomas G. Blomberg
Gordon P. Waldo
Lisa C. Burcroff

Since 1983, a major program movement literally has exploded across the United States in response to unprecedented inmate population growth. This program movement has been variously termed intensive surveillance, house arrest, community control, electronic surveillance, home incarceration or home confinement. This paper considers the development of this movement and identifies some of the different operational features and implications of home confinement programs. Included among the major findings is the tendency nationwide to equate and implement home confinement using electronic surveillance measures. Home confinement without electronic surveillance is the exception rather than the rule. In assessing implications, it is argued that in the future electronic surveillance measures may well be extended into a number of other areas of the criminal justice system as well as society at large. It is concluded that electronic surveillance may soon become the new strategy of social control without empirical justification for this strategy having been established or some of the potential negative consequences identified.

169

INTRODUCTION

During the 1960s and '70s a series of community correctional reform programs emerged as alternatives to jails, prisons and formal criminal justice system processing. Halfway houses, residential centers, group homes, specialized probation services, diversion and deinstitutionaliza- tion programs were promoted as less costly and more effective alternatives to the traditional institution-based criminal justice system. Yet, despite the national proliferation of these various community correctional pro- grams, U.S. jail and prison populations continued to increase with un- precedented growth in the early '80s. A major program movement that has emerged in response to this recent inmate population growth has been variously termed intensive surveillance, house arrest, community con- trol, electronic surveillance, home incarceration or home confinement.

Florida was the first state to implement a statewide home confinement program. This program is aimed at diverting nonviolent offenders from prison by providing around-the-clock surveillance of these offenders. Cur- rently, the federal prison system and numerous state and local jurisdic- tions have or are in the process of implementing home confinement pro- grams. With the exception of Florida, Georgia and Massachusetts, the state and local home confinement programs are employing various forms of electronic monitoring devices in their offender surveillance activities. (States using home confinement with electronic monitoring include: California, Colorado, Idaho, Illinois, Kentucky, Michigan, New Jersey, New Mexico, New York, Oklahoma, Oregon, Utah and Virginia.) This means that most offenders being placed on home confinement are sub- ject to some form of 24 hour electronically monitored home surveillance.

Inexplicably, the terms, ''home confinement'' and ''electronic surveillance'' are frequently used as synonyms in much of the home con- finement literature, as well as by correction agencies. To elaborate, in re- cent correspondence with correction administrators around the country concerning home confinement, the respondents frequently assumed, although the letters clearly specified to the contrary, that the questions being asked related to the electronic hardware used for surveillance. Many of their responses also equated home confinement with electronic monitor- ing. As becomes clear in the discussion that follows, jurisdictions can have home confinement without electronic surveillance, and electronic monitor- ing can logically be extended far beyond home confinement.

Regardless of this confusion in terminology, in a manner similar to previous experiences with community corrections programs in the '60s and '70s, it now appears that home confinement and electronic surveillance are fast becoming accepted national crime control policies.

This paper identifies some of the operational features of home confinement and electronic surveillance programs, and considers some of the implications of these operations.

BACKGROUND OF HOME CONFINEMENT
AND ELECTRONIC SURVEILLANCE
PROGRAM DEVELOPMENT

The U.S. General Accounting Office (1984) reported that in 1983 the
number of state and federal prisoners grew by 24,000 to reach a record
number of 438,830 inmates at year's end. The report included projections
indicating that 528,193 inmates would be imprisoned in the year 1990,
and that U.S. prison capacity for 1990 would be 419,869. The U.S. Bureau
of Justice Statistics (1985) reported that 26,618 prisoners were added to
the prison rolls in 1984. This increase brought the total growth in the prison
population since 1980 to more than 134,000 inmates, or a 40 percent increase in a four year period.

The Bureau of Justice Statistics report specified two consequences
associated with the significant growth in the U.S. prison population, namely: (1) a significant increase in state prisoners held in local jails (moving
from 8,073 in 1983 to 11,555 in 1984); and (2) a dramatic increase of $1.2
billion in spending by state correctional authorities, for an all-time high
of $7.2 billion.

It is from this context of extremes—prison and jail overcrowding, growing fiscal crisis, and a simultaneous acceleration in the public's mandate
to get tough on criminals and reduce taxes—that home confinement and
electronic surveillance programs have emerged.

NON-ELECTRONIC MONITORED HOME CONFINEMENT: THE
FLORIDA EXAMPLE

In 1983, Florida implemented the first statewide home confinement program. To date, Florida's home confinement program has involved almost
5,000 offenders, making it the largest program in the country. Florida's
home confinement officers conduct daily intensive supervision and
surveillance of offenders even on evenings and weekends. According to
Florida statute, these officers operate with a maximum caseload of 20.
The basic conditions prescribed (State of Florida, 1983) for home confinement cases include the following:

1. Report to home confinement officer at least four times a week, or,

if employed part-time, report daily.

2. Perform at least 140 hours of public service work, without pay, as directed by the home confinement officer.

3. Remain confined to residence except for approved employment, public service work, or other special activities specifically approved by the home confinement officer.

4. Make monthly restitution payments for a specified total amount.

5. Submit to and pay for urinalysis, breathalyzer or blood specimen tests at any time as requested by the home confinement officer or other professional staff to determine possible use of alcohol, drugs, or other controlled substances.

6. Maintain an hourly account of all activities in a daily log to be submitted to the home confinement officer upon request.

7. Participate in self-improvement programs as determined by the court or home confinement officer.

8. Promptly and truthfully answer all inquiries of the court or home confinement officer, and allow the officer to visit home, employer, or elsewhere.

9. For sex offenders, the court requires, as a special condition of home confinement, the release of treatment information to the home confinement officer or the court.

The sentencing judge or parole commission determines the exact terms and conditions of individual home confinement cases, which can be later modified or rescinded.

There are three categories of offenders eligible for home confinement:

1. Those found guilty of non-forcible felonies (or "others" who are deemed appropriate by a sentencing judge),

2. Probationers charged with technical or misdemeanor violations, and

3. Parolees charged with technical or misdemeanor violations.

Following an offender's placement on home confinement, a needs assessment is conducted to develop an individualized home confinement plan. The plan and its objectives include specific sanctions and restraints to be imposed on the offender while on home confinement, and other requirements such as participation in self-improvement programs, along with the target dates for initiating and completing the requirements. The home confinement officer is authorized to provide "firm guidance" and supervision throughout implementation of the plan. The plan is to be recorded and signed by the officer and the offender and kept in the offender's case file.

Home confinement can be terminated by a court order, with a maximum term of two years in the program. If it is determined that an offender has made satisfactory adjustment and completed the plan requirements before expiration of the sentence, the court can be petitioned to transfer the offender to regular probation supervision. Or, in the case of a parole violator on home confinement, the parole commission can be petitioned to assign the offender to regular parole supervision. It is also possible to petition the court for early termination of home confinement without further supervision in those cases where it is decided that sufficient adjustment has been made and all program plan requirements have been met. It should be noted that, to date, few parole cases have been placed on home confinement.

A primary operational procedure that has evolved in Florida's home confinement program is team surveillance. According to officers, this enables them to keep the offenders "off guard," and provides personnel for evening and weekend surveillance. The team approach reflects, in part, the strong emphasis of home confinement officers on their supervision and surveillance function. The State of Florida is responding to this emphasis by training home confinement officers in surveillance as well as self-defense, search and seizure, and legal liability.

In a recent statewide survey of home confinement officers, offenders, and offenders' families, a majority of the officers favored being armed (Blomberg and Bullock, 1984), but at this time the state has not made a final decision on this issue. The officers now carry police flashlights for protection, but concern over officer safety continues to be voiced across the state. Several other interesting findings were reported in the survey. For example, home confinement officers indicated that most offenders were able to either find new employment or retain their previous employment while on home confinement. Moreover, employers reported positive experiences with the offenders they hired, and unemployment among home confinement cases was reported to be very rare.

A positive result reported by spouses of offenders was that their husbands were providing their families with full paychecks, instead of the previous pattern of only a part of the paycheck going toward family expenses. Further, offenders on home confinement and family members alike reported more interest and participation by the offender in the family and home. Home confinement officers reported that married and more mature offenders had an easier time in successfully adapting to the requirements of home confinement. In direct contrast, however, younger and less mature offenders frequently were unable to successfully fulfill home confinement's program requirements.

ELECTRONICALLY MONITORED HOME CONFINEMENT

Among the state and local jurisdictions using electronic monitors for the surveillance of offenders in their homes, some programs accept felons, but most are targeted for nonviolent misdemeanants. All of these programs require that offenders placed on home confinement be thoroughly screened, and participation is reported to be voluntary. "Voluntary" participation is aimed, in part, at alleviating constitutional issues or conflicts. Generally, offenders on electronically monitored home confinement are assigned to officers who set the rules and guidelines for the offender (and his or her family) to follow. At any time throughout the confinement process the offender may elect to quit the program and go to jail or prison for a prescribed amount of time. (For elaboration of these points see Ford and Schmidt, 1985.)

Typically, offenders in the program are fitted with an electronic surveillance device that is connected to some form of telephone monitor in the home. At present there are at least nine different monitors on the market, all but two of them involving the use of a telephone in one form or another.

ELECTRONIC SURVEILLANCE AND THE EXTENSION OF CONTROL

Home confinement is now being equated with electronic surveillance not only by the public by by correctional policymakers and practitioners too. Despite the experiences of Florida, Massachusetts and Georgia with non-electronically monitored home confinement, most states and local jurisdictions are being drawn to a home confinement approach emphasizing electronic monitoring. The perception is that this technology can solve a series of complex and interrelated problems associated with appropriate and effective offender supervision. Clearly, prior experience has demonstrated repeatedly that narrowly conceived solutions to the complex problem of crime control tend to be unsuccessful and frequently result in unanticipated consequences. While it may be that under some circumstances electronic surveillance is an effective or appropriate alternative to imprisonment or jail, we have just begun to think about these circumstances, let alone responsibly evaluate this evolving correctional strategy.

Nonetheless, it appears that during the next several years electronic surveillance strategies will likely proliferate. There are many potential, if not proven, uses and objectives for electronic surveillance in the criminal justice system in addition to home confinement. At the present time the technology does not exist to accomplish many of these objectives; however, with the rapid pace of technological advancement it is likely that the capacity for various forms of electronic surveillance will be greatly expanded in the near future. While the authors of this paper do not advocate the use of electronic surveillance as described below, it is likely that because of the precedent set in home confinement programs that many of these uses will be explored and implemented in the near future despite the legal, constitutional, ethical, moral and empirical issues this technology raises.

Among the possible new uses of electronic surveillance in addition to home confinement would be monitoring the movements of probationers or parolees. It is accepted by many in corrections that a major reason for failure on probation or parole is contact with bad associates and the use of alcohol or drugs. Electronic surveillance could provide a system of control whereby probationers and parolees are more closely monitored in order to reduce these undesirable contacts and thereby reduce failure on probation or parole.

Similarly, a common reason for failure in programs is the offender's desire for alcohol or the wish to spend several hours with a girlfriend or boyfriend on the way back to the institution after a day of work or study. These potential sources of trouble for the offender could be avoided if a system of electronic surveillance were in place so that a supervisor would know where the releasee was located at any time.

Electronic surveillance also has potential for use within prisons and jails in order to keep track of the location and activities of inmates. Many problems are created in institutions by inmates who are in the wrong place at the wrong time. A monitoring system that could track and record the activities of inmates could avoid many of these problems. In addition, electronic monitoring could reduce the opportunities for escape from an institution or make an inmate's capture easier if an escape did occur.

There are some whom might suggest other categories of people in contact with the criminal justice system—not directly under correctional supervision—who might benefit from electronic surveillance. In many states there are restrictions placed on ex-offenders who have finished serving their sentences. For example, they may be required to register their addresses with law enforcement officials whenever they move into a community, or they may be prohibited from practicing specific occupations, or they may be prohibited from purchasing or owning firearms. Electronic surveillance may be helpful in assuring that these requirements are adhered to by ex-offenders.

Quasi-criminal justice clientele participate in self-help programs for alcohol and drug abusers, gamblers, or people with sexual dysfunctions. Failures in these programs often result from the temptation to revert to the former behavior pattern when not in the presence of the group. Many of these groups provide support for their members when they become aware of a crisis situation that might cause the member to revert. A system of electronic monitoring could be established so that the self-help group would be alerted when a member approached an area known to be problematic for the individual.

If we momentarily ignore issues related to constitutionality, electronic monitoring may also be useful in reducing the number of crimes committed by people on bail awaiting trial for an earlier crime. This problem is deemed sufficiently severe in some areas that preventive detention programs are used so that potential offenders are not eligible for bail. Electronic monitoring could become a condition of bail, or at least of "release on recognizance." This principle could be extended (again, constitutionality temporarily aside) to include suspects "known" by the police to have committed a crime but against whom the evidence is insufficient or inadmissible, leading to the suspect's release. Many of these suspects return to the community to commit new crimes. Electronic surveillance could be used to deter these suspects from committing new crimes, or might lead to capture if they do so.

Some might suggest another extension of this process to include crime prevention. If a system could be developed for predicting delinquent or criminal tendencies, then the individuals so identified could be electronically monitored as a deterrent.

In addition to the criminal justice system, electronic surveillance has social control potential in many other areas. For example, people with infectious diseases such as AIDS could be more effectively controlled with electronic surveillance. The mentally ill or handicapped could be prevented from harming themselves or others when they wander away from their homes or institutions. People identified as having suicidal tendencies could also be fitted with electronic devices for their protection. Similar protection could be extended to the senile elderly, young children and teenagers.

The monitoring technology could also be used by employers concerned about employee productivity, coaches desiring reliable curfew checks of their players, teachers wanting to keep track of their students, and supervisors in any other type of institutional setting. At the personal end of the continuum, the husband or wife who wants to keep track of a spouse suspected of being unfaithful might adopt an "electronic chastity belt."

There are numerous other uses for electronic surveillance that could be readily "justified," and the limitations of its use are more a function of our imagination than the technology. Obviously, such broad use of electronic surveillance poses interrelated questions involving legal and constitutional rights, the proper use of surveillance in a democratic society, the role of the criminal justice system, and explicit criteria that need to be met before employing electronic surveillance. The rapid growth of legal and constitutional issues related to electronic monitoring is perhaps best demonstrated by the fact that textbooks are starting to appear on this subject, such as James Carr's *The Law of Electronic Surveillance* (1986).

While it cannot be covered in any detail at this point, there is considerable debate concerning the constitutionality of the electronic monitoring of convicted offenders, not to mention the other categories noted above. Most jurisdictions have reasoned that the use of electronic monitoring of offenders does not violate the U.S. Constitution because:

1. participation in the program is voluntary (i.e., involves "informed consent"), and thus the offender knows and understands the conditions and responsibilities of participation, and

2. since the participant is a convicted criminal, he has no reasonable expectation of privacy.

However, the question of informed consent becomes very muddled when consideration is given to voluntary choice without coercion. Specifically, does coercion exist when an offender is offered the choice of serving a sentence in prison versus electronic monitoring in the home? Currently, one of the main criticisms of electronic monitors is that they violate the fourth amendment protection against unreasonable searches and seizures. Case law in this area is extremely limited because the use of electronic monitors is so recent. The fourth amendment protects against unreasonable search and seizure of private premises and property. Corrections personnel often assert that because the offender waives this right in order to participate in the program, he has no right to expect privacy. No doubt there will be considerable litigation on these questions in the near future.

SUMMARY AND DISCUSSION

The purpose of this paper has been to identify and assess some of the salient operations and implications of the home confinement and electronic surveillance movement. A major operational feature of home confinement has been the demonstrated tendency nationwide to equate and subsequently implement home confinement with electronic surveillance measures. Home confinement without electronic surveillance is the exception instead of the rule. In assessing some of the implications of the electronic surveillance movement, it was suggested that electronic surveillance measures may well be extended into a number of other areas of the criminal justice system and beyond. Electronic surveillance may represent a new strategy of social control for the 1980s. Similar to previous experience with community corrections programs in the '60s and '70s, home confinement with electronic surveillance is becoming a national crime control strategy before empirical justification for this approach has been established.

Electronic surveillance and other related community-based correctional strategies demonstrate the changing character of social control in American society. Cohen (1985) argues that the community corrections reform movement represents an extension of discipline from such total institutions as jail, prisons, reformatories and asylums to the broader community. The potential for expanded uses of electronic surveillance exemplifies Cohen's decentralization of social control argument. In a similar vein, Messinger (1982) argues that community corrections programs and related decentralized methods of control signal "the coming of a minimum security society" in which an ever-increasing proportion of the base population could become subject to some form of control or surveillance. Clearly, such implications, and the explosive proliferation of various home confinement programs using electronic surveillance, demonstrate the immediate need for detailed empirical studies that are sensitive to the complexity and potentially mixed results of these programs. Meanwhile, even in the absence of empirical evidence specifying exactly what home confinement with electronic surveillance can and cannot do and for whom, the uses of this technology could extend well beyond the criminal offender.

REFERENCES

Blomberg, Thomas G. and Carol Bullock (1984). *Community Control Job-Task Analysis.* Report to the Florida Department of Corrections, Tallahassee, FL.

Burcroff, Lisa (1986). Information received while at the U.S. National Institute of Justice, Washington, DC.

Carr, James G. (1986). *The Law of Electronic Surveillance.* New York: Clark Boardman.

Cohen, Stanley (1985). *Visions of Social Control.* Cambridge, MA: Polity Press.

Ford, D. and Anne Schmidt (1985). "Electronically Monitored Home Confinement." *NIJ Reports.* Washington, DC: U.S. National Institute of Justice.

Messinger, Sheldon (1982). Personal correspondence.

Schmidt, Anne (1986). "Electronic Monitoring Equipment." Washington, DC: U.S. National Institute of Justice.

State of Florida (1983). *An Implementation Manual for Community Control.*

Tallahassee, FL: Florida Department of Corrections.

U.S. Bureau of Justice Statistics (1985). *Prisoners in 1984.* Bureau of Justice Statistics Annual Report. Washington, DC.

U.S. General Accounting Office (1984). *Report to the Honorable Arlen Specter, United States Senate.* Washington, DC.

Palm Beach County's In-House Arrest Work Release Program

by
Palm Beach County,
Florida Sheriff's Department

This chapter has been adapted for Intermediate Punishments *from a report prepared by and for the Palm Beach County Sheriff's Department. It differs from other contributions in that it is a self report of the problems of institutional overcrowding as they are perceived and addressed by local law enforcement officials. Using the discretion provided under Florida law, Sheriff Richard Wille and Judge Edward Garrison created a program to meet their community's needs. In Palm Beach County, home confinement serves as a transition from work release to the community, and as an intermediate punishment for a diverse group of offenders.*

Richard P. Wille, Sheriff of Palm Beach County, Florida, became the first law enforcement official to sanction the use of electronic surveillance equipment to monitor the presence of sentenced inmates in their own homes. The decision to implement a pilot program in December 1984 resulted from meetings with Palm Beach County Judge Edward Garrison in an effort to solve overcrowding in the Palm Beach County jail system.

There are several major factors contributing to the jail overcrowding problem in Palm Beach County. First, Sheriff Wille is responsible for law enforcement in an area equal in size to the State of Delaware. Second, Palm Beach County is experiencing a population explosion that is one of the largest in the United States and is forecast to continue through the remainder of this decade and well into the next. Palm Beach is a premier resort area that unfortunately attracts the criminal element as well as vacationers. In addition to the climate, the criminal element is attracted by the close proximity of the Caribbean and South American drug trafficking centers. Florida has 8,426 miles of tidal coastline, second only to Alaska, making law enforcement a responsibility of staggering proportions for Sheriff Wille's office and other law enforcement agencies.

How the System Works

Today's advanced electronic technology allows a system to monitor the presence of an individual who is to be in his/her home at a predetermined time. It is ideal for inmates who qualify for a work release program. This system consists of the following three major components:

Transmitter. A battery-powered water and moisture proof transmitter is securely fastened by riveted plastic straps just above the inmate's ankle. The transmitter emits a signal at regular intervals with a maximum range of approximately 100 feet.

Receiver/Dialer. A receiver/dialer that connects to a 110A/C power outlet and standard phone jack is installed in the inmate's home. This unit monitors the signal fromt he tansmitter and automatically dials the host computer, describing the time the inmate goes beyond the range of the signal, or returns within the range of the signal. Also, this unit will automatically dial the host computer when it has been tampered with, moved, unplugged or returned to the A/C power source. If the telephone line has been cut or disconnected, preventing the dialer from calling in, the message is stored until such time the unit is reconnected to the A/C power and telephone; at that time it will send a delayed message describing the actual time of each activity.

Host Computer. A small personal computer (PC), complete with disk drive, video screen and printer, is installed at the Stockade Division of the Palm Beach Sheriff's Office. The PC interprets the incoming messages based on the stored logic of the In-House Arrest Program. This program contains the inmate's personal data, home address, telephone number, business address, supervisor's name and telephone number, and his weekly schedule, which reflects the times he is authorized to be away from home. There is no Sunday work and no work on three major holidays— Christmas, Thanksgiving and New Year's Day. A violation message will be printed immediately when a "Left Home" or "Returned Home" message is received for an unauthorized time. Also, a violation message will be printed when the PC receives a signal indicating the receiver/dialer has been tampered with, moved, unplugged, or the phone lines have been cut or disconnected. The PC is on-line 24 hours a day automatically updating records based on the messages received. The system allows easy access for adding or deleting inmate records, generating daily summaries, or making inquiries.

All violations are reviewed and verified by the officers assigned to the program, either by telephoning the individual, or visiting his home or job site. Inmates who commit a serious violation must be brought before Lt. Eugene Garcia, who determines what action is to be taken.

Inmate Selection Criteria

Currently, Sheriff Richard P. Wille shoulders all of the responsibility for the inmates selected and placed in the In-House Arrest Work Release Program. To be considered for the program, inmates must first complete a portion of their sentences in the traditional work release program, where they must return to the institution each night after working in the community. In addition to a good track record, inmates who volunteer for the program are subject to additional background checks. Sentenced inmates with the following charges are not considered for the In-House Arrest Work Release Program: murder, rape, child molestation, armed robbery, drug charges, sexual related crimes, and vehicular homicide. (Consideration will be given when the victim's family submits written consent.) Each inmate must have residence in Palm Beach County with a telephone.

Program Components

Sponsors. A sponsor, such as a spouse, parent or friend, is desirable but not necessary. Inmates who have their own residences and live alone have been placed in the program and have successfully completed their sentences. Prior to leaving the institution, each inmate and his sponsor are interviewed by Lt. Garcia so that he may review and explain each "condition of agreement" listed on the contract the inmate must sign. The purpose of the meeting is to prevent any misunderstanding by the inmate or any member of his household and give each the opportunity to reject the program at this time.

Contract. The contract contains the inmate's name, address, employment data, serial numbers of electronic equipment and authorized hours away from his place of residence. It also contains the per diem and weekly inspection schedule. The contract contains 14 conditions of agreement that each inmate must abide by.

Per Diem and Inspection. Each inmate must return to the institution on

the last work day of his/her week. At this time, each inmate must pay
$9.00 for each day in the system. Also, each inmate must have his/her
transmitter inspected by the officer on duty to determine the condition
of the straps holding the transmitter in place.

Benefits to Inmates. Electronic surveillance offers an alternative to incarceration by placing selected offenders in their own homes. Incarceration of a nonviolent offender is not the answer and may even be counterproductive, not only for the individual, but also for society. This program
allows offenders to maintain their jobs, thus enabling them to support their
families, pay court costs, and to make restitution to the victims.

Highlights of 1985

The following analysis covers the period from December 14, 1984
through December 31, 1985. During this time 87 offenders were in the
In-House Arrest Program, including 85 sentenced inmates who
volunteered for the work release program and two pretrial offenders who
were court ordered. The court ordered offenders were two women found
to be suffering from AIDS. The 87 offenders accumulated 4,816 days in
the program for an average of 55 days each. One inmate successfully completed 311 days, while there were 14 others who had more than 100 days
each.

This system has been a success; only three inmates caused serious problems. One escaped and two were arrested on new charges. The serious
problems represent only 3 percent of the total. Sixty-one offenders have
been released after successfully completing their sentences. Lt. Garcia
removed nine with lesser violations, such as loss of job, loss of transportation, problems at home, etc. The only problem peculiar to the In-House
Arrest Work Release Program is the "problems at home" violation; all
other problems may, and have, occurred in the traditional work release
program.

Over 60% of the inmates placed in the In-House Arrest Work Release
Program were convicted felons. Their crimes included: grand theft, ut-
tering a forged prescription, obtaining a controlled substance by fraud,
forgery, burglary, aggravated battery, robbery, aggravated assault, possession of a concealed weapon, second degree arson, DWI-accident with in-
jury, dealing in stolen property, and fraud.

As for the two women with AIDS, it was felt that incarceration should
be avoided if at all possible. In the first case, Judge Garrison called Lt.
Garcia and inquired about placing the woman on "house arrest" to
alleviate the problem for all concerned. Lt. Garcia agreed to put this
woman in her own home and monitor her presence through use of the

electronic surveillance equipment, where she completed 40 days of house arrest prior to her appearance. The dramatic change in this woman, both physically and mentally, is testimony to the rehabilitative potential of electronic surveillance and an alternative to incarceration. This woman was thin, haggard, and very depressed when placed in the program, as compared to the person who, 40 days later, had gained 25 pounds and displayed a great deal of enthusiasm for life. The second woman had a deep rooted drug habit that prevented her from coping with her problems. The courts, with the backing of her family, later placed this woman in a medical facility where she received help for both the drug problem and AIDS. Both of these women expressed gratitude for being placed in their own homes with the love and care of their family. Without the availability of electronic surveillance, these two women would have faced incarceration and isolation.

Court Ordered Community Control

Florida statutes provide the courts with guidelines for the future use of electronic surveillance equipment as an alternative to incarceration for sentenced offenders and selected pretrial detainees. The following excerpts are taken from some of these statutes.

Community Control (FS 948.001): "Community control means a form of intensive supervised custody in the community, including surveillance on weekends and holidays, administered by officers with restricted case loads. Community control is an individualized program in which the freedom of an offender is restricted within the community, home, or non-institutional residential placement, and specific sanctions are imposed and enforced."

Disposition and Sentencing: Alternatives (FS 921.187): "The following alternatives for the disposition of criminal cases shall be used in a manner which will best serve the needs of society, which will punish criminal offenders, and which will provide the opportunity for rehabilitation. A court may:

(3) Place a felony offender into community control requiring intensive supervision and surveillance pursuant to chapter 948."

Presentence Investigation Reports (FS 921.231): "Any circuit court in the state, when the defendant in a criminal felony case has been found guilty or has entered a plea of nolo contendre or guilty, shall, and in misdemeanor cases in its discretion may, refer the case to the Department of Corrections for investigation and recommendation. It shall be the duty of the department to make a report in writing to the circuit court at a specified time prior to sentencing, depending upon the circumstances of the offender and the offense. Said report shall include:

(g) Information about the environment to which the offender might return or to which he could be sent should a sentence of non-incarceration or community supervision be imposed by the court."

Community Control Programs (FS 948.10): "The program shall offer the courts an alternative, community-based method to punish an offender in lieu of incarceration when the offender is a member of one of the following target groups:

a. Probation violators charged with technical violations or misdemeanor violations.

b. Parole violators charged with technical violations or misdemeanor violations.

c. Individuals found guilty of felonies, who, due to their criminal backgrounds for the seriousness of the offenses, would not be placed on regular probation."

Local Offender Advisory Councils (FS 948.90): "It is the intent of the Legislature that cities and counties or combinations thereof have the option to develop, establish and maintain community programs to provide the judicial system with community alternatives for certain non-violent offenders who may require less than institutional custody but more than probation supervision pursuant to this chapter. It is further intended that such programs provide increased opportunities for offenders to make restitution to victims of crime through financial reimbursement of community service, while promoting efficiency and economy in the delivery of correctional services."

Return on Investment

The following is a comparison of the original cost of the system versus the return on investment as of January 1, 1986.

Hardware and Software:

1 Software package (In-House Arrest Program)	$ 3,500
1 PC computer, W/disk drive, printer & screen	$ 4,000
1 PC communications panel (linkage for WATS)	$ 6,000
45 Receiver/dialers & transmitters @$795.	$35,775
Total Cost..	$ 49,275

Payback as of January 1, 1986:

Daily charge per inmate	$ 9
Total man days to date	4,765
Total Payback ($9 x 4,765).....................	$ 42,885
Percent of return of investment	87%

(The WATS line charges are buried in the overall 800 line charges for the Sheriff's Office, making it difficult to arrive at a definitive cost for the WATS line. However, future plans to convert to FX lines will reduce the cost of telephone calls.)

Conclusion

The concept of electronically monitored home incarceration is a boon to the American taxpayer in view of the facts:

U.S. jail populations have more than doubled in the past 10 years.

A new prison cell costs anywhere from $25,000 to $75,000.

It costs $40 to $60 per day to house one inmate.

It costs up to $1,600 per year for each person on probation.

$7 billion is allocated for new prisons in the United States.

There are several hundred thousand sentenced inmates in the United States serving one year or less who may be screened for possible acceptance into a home incarceration program. If only 1,200 of these inmates were selected from each state and placed in the type of system introduced by the Palm Beach Sheriff's Office, this concept could reduce inmate housing costs per year by $876 million and produce a cash flow of $197 million. In addition, these inmates would be able to support their families, assume their own medical responsibilities, reduce the cost of welfare and food stamp programs, pay court costs and make restitution to the victims of crime.

The concept of in-house arrest is a proven success. Already the system has been adopted by agencies from coast to coast, and in other countries. Second and third generation equipment has been developed. Keen competition in this billion-dollar field will ensure an excellent product. This marks an important breakthrough in the treatment of the nonviolent first-time offender, for whom incarceration has proved to be no solution. The future of this concept looks very bright.

Home Incarceration with Electronic Monitoring in Kenton County, Kentucky: An Evaluation

by
J. Robert Lilly
Richard A. Ball
Jennifer Wright

This report provides an evaluation of a home incarceration program with electronic monitoring in Kenton County, Kentucky. The data presented are for May 1, 1985 through mid-December 1986. The report is organized into three major divisions: (1) the history of home incarceration in Kentucky, (2) findings from the pilot study, and (3) a discussion of "net widening," home incarceration for chronic misdemeanants and Kentucky's 1986 enabling legislation. The findings indicate that most people sentenced were males charged with non-violent offenses, including drunk driving and violation of child support orders. A high percentage of the offenders had prior convictions, some with jail sentences. Home incarceration does not appear to have expanded the "criminal justice net."

HISTORY

In 1984, a Kentucky General Assembly bill (Ky. H.B. 8.305) to give statutory support to home incarceration with electronic monitoring was deliberately killed by its sponsors. The bill had resulted from nearly two years of extensive groundwork, including examination by interested scholars (Ball and Lilly 1983a; 1983b; 1984a; 1984b; 1985; 1986a; 1986b; 1987), the generation of bipartisan sponsorship within the General Assembly, and endorsements by the Kentucky Fraternal Order of Police, the Mental Health Association of Northern Kentucky, the Kentucky Jailers Association and numerous other civic groups. The bill was also endorsed by some of the press (*Kentucky Post,* February 15, 1984), which also provided extensive coverage of the bill while it was in committee (Calhoun, 1984; 1985a; 1985b; Straub 1984; 1985; 1986).

The bill's sponsors killed it as a political strategy because it became embroiled in a tax reform controversy that threatened its passage. Interest in the bill continued, however, aided by a state department of corrections request for a pilot study. At the same time, supporters of the bill sought to implement home incarceration and electronic monitoring in a manner that would not require legislative action (Ball and Lilly, 1984a; 1984b).

A receptive audience for home incarceration and electronic monitoring was found in Kenton County, where the judge-executive and the county jailer were attempting to comply with court injunctions to reduce jail overcrowding (Neikirk, 1984). Between early November 1984 and late January 1985, Kenton County officials decided to try home incarceration with electronic monitoring devices similar to the equipment developed by Corrections Services, Inc. of West Palm Beach, Florida.

The 20-page agreement between the county district court, the county jailer and the state department of corrections provided that the pilot project would explore alternatives to incarceration for selected misdemeanants who posed a minimal risk to the community. It also specified the program's rules and regulations, including an explanation of the conditions of the program to the offender, the responsibilities of the court, presentence investigator and the county jailer, a description of the monitoring equipment and a copy of the forms to be used for each case.

Generally, the agreement was more oriented to the interests of the court than of the offender, even though participation was voluntary. For instance, the agreement did not indicate that an offender could petition the court for home incarceration, nor did it sanction the initiation of home incarceration by an offender's attorney. At no point did the agreement indicate that the offender could petition to be removed from the program; neither was this option mentioned for an offender's spouse or family.

Presumably, offenders could be released from home incarceration only if they successfully completed the sentence or if they violated the agreement and were "terminated."

FINDINGS

The data collected were from interviews and examinations of the offender files held by the state's presentence investigation staff. Those interviewed included each offender who accepted home incarceration as a sentence and his immediate family, usually a spouse. An unmarried offender's parents, and sometimes the offender's friends, were also interviewed. In addition, judges, presentence investigation/probation officers, the county jail staff who worked with the home incarceration program, the county treasurer, fiscal court staff and the program coordinator were interviewed. The files were examined for prior charges and convictions.

The primary reason for this evaluation was to "determine if home incarceration will alleviate, in a cost effective manner, overcrowding in Kenton County's jail" (Lilly, 1985:1). The answer is that home incarceration

Table 1

Expenses

Direct Costs (Kenton County)		
Hardware	$ 6,987.00	
Software	17,975.00	
Postage	1,301.00	
Phone	100.00	
Computer Training	680.00	
		$27,043.00
Indirect Costs (Kenton County)		
15% of Salary for Administrative		
Assistant (May 1985-December, 1986)	$ 5,500.00	
(Dept. of Corrections)		
½ Salary for P/P Officer	10,000.00	
Mileage @ .18 per mile	25.00	
		$15,525.00
	TOTAL:	$42,568.00

Table 2

Direct Costs and Limited Indirect Costs Comparisons		
Direct Costs		
Hardware	$6,987.00	
Software	17,975.00	
Postage	1,301.00	
Phone	100.00	
Training	680.00	
		$27,043.00
Indirect Costs		
Mileage	25.00	$ 25.00
	Total:	$27,068.00

did not substantially reduce the jail's overcrowding. With only 40 people referred and approved by P.S.I. (Pre-Sentence Investigation) for home confinement, too few offenders were directed to this alternative to produce a significant change in the jail population or create a positive economic impact on the jail budget.

This does not mean home incarceration had no effect. In fact, 1,702 days of incarceration occurred outside of the jail through the use of home incarceration with electronic monitoring.

In the words of one of the judges in Kenton County, "Any time you can save a bed-day in jail, you have done something positive for the criminal system." But what did 1,702 days of incarceration outside of the jail cost? This information is presented in Table 1.

A total of $42,568 was required to incarcerate 35 people for 1,702 days outside of the jail. In contrast, at a daily maintenance fee of $26 per person for jail incarceration, 1,702 days would have cost $44,252. This means that jail incarceration for 1,702 days would cost $1,684 more than home incarceration with electronic monitoring. However, this figure is misleading, because salaries for the home incarceration program's administrative assistant and probation and parole officers did not require expenditure of additional funds (see Table 2).

Thus, as Table 2 indicates, the total direct and indirect costs can be reduced from $42,568 to $27,068, a figure $15,500 less than jail time. This means that home incarceration has the potential for costing less than jail incarceration.

Kenton County also received income from home incarceration with electronic monitoring. During the time of the research, a total of $6,377 was received from 83 percent of the 35 people sentenced to home incarceration. The fee structure was based on a maximum of 25 percent of the offender's net weekly household income. Individuals with less than $100 net income per week paid no fees.

Expectations and Results

The Kentucky Department of Corrections had three objectives for home incarceration (Lilly 1985):

A.   Protect the citizenry of the commonwealth with a minimum of financial burden on its citizens.

B.   Assist the county judge-executives and jailers in their administration of jail depopulation, as well as providing an option for district court judges in their administration of justice.

C.   Aid the offenders in accepting their responsibilities to their families and the community through treatment programs, restitution, community service, job training, and employment.

Protection. The issue of protection was approached in two ways: (1) Did the individual sentenced to home incarceration comply with the rules established for this form of incarceration? (2) Were additional crimes committed during home incarceration?

Three people did not comply with the conditions of home incarceration; however, only two of these individuals (5.7 percent) were removed from the program for direct rule violations. Both were "caught" by the monitoring equipment *and* corroborative evidence, and were returned to the Kenton County Jail. The third person was removed from the program because he was unable to maintain the cost of a telephone. It is concluded that home incarceration with electronic monitoring does help protect the citizens.

Interdepartmental Assistance. The second objective has two parts: (1) Assist the County Judge Executive and jailers in their administration of jail depopulation, and (2) provide an option for district court judges in their administration of justice. In practice, the first part depended largely if not entirely on the second part. Depopulating the jail depended upon judges employing home incarceration as a sentencing alternative. In the words of the jailer, "home incarceration was not used enough on the front end"; i.e., it was not used enough as an initial sentence to depopulate the jail.

Neither, according to the jailer, was home incarceration used enough as a condition of work release outside jail, which also depends on the approval of a district judge. According to the jailer, the judges were too conservative in their use of home incarceration. Nevertheless, the jailer liked home incarceration and wished to use it as a condition of work release without the approval of a judge.

Each of the three district judges in Kenton County voiced support for the program, and each judge sentenced someone to home incarceration. However, there was very little consistency in sentencing philosophy. One judge used home incarceration as an additional option before sentencing to jail rather than as an alternative.

Another judge stated he was "just not into home incarceration all that much" because he prefers giving a lot of offenders jail time, even if it is short. It appeared to him that probation and parole officers preferred to have individuals sentenced to home incarceration for 30 days or longer, which seemed inconsistent with the time they would have to spend in jail if sentenced to 30 days. (Because of jail overcrowding, a person sentenced to 30 days in jail would be out in 10 days.) In addition, this judge reported that he had offered home incarceration to two individuals who refused it, saying they would rather spend 10 days in jail, have the jail feed them and pay no fees, rather than have to stay at home for 30 days, feed themselves and pay fees.

Another judge agreed with this reasoning, saying: "As long as the jail is crowded, home incarceration cannot be tested because jail is a *good* deal" (emphasis in the original). He stated further, "If someone *needs* to be locked up, they should go to jail. Home incarceration is just not the same idea as jail incarceration." Like the jailer, this judge recommended that home incarceration with electronic monitoring continue. The other judges agreed with this recommendation.

It is concluded that district court judges did not use home incarceration as an alternative to jail. One judge thought of it as a "prelude" to jail, another thought of it as "not incarceration," while the third thought of it as a sentencing option worth continuing. Thus far home incarceration has been used conservatively in Kenton County. It has not been seriously tested as an alternative to jail incarceration.

Offender Aid. The third major objective was to assist offenders in accepting their responsibilities to their families and the community through treatment programs, restitution, community services, job training, and employment. The findings related to this objective are rather positive, but it is not so clear that home incarceration is responsible for the outcomes. For example, 63 percent of those sentenced in the pilot project were employed, indicating that a sense of responsibility to oneself and family existed prior to the home incarceration sentence. Compared to only 16 percent (17/104) of those in the Kenton County Jail who were employed at the same time in work release programs, those in home incarceration evidenced a greater sense of responsibility. It should be noted that offenders sentenced to home incarceration were not required to work. In fact, approximately 37 percent of the offenders were not employed. (Caution must be exercised with this comparison because the base for calculating the 16 percent included both misdemeanants and felons, while all of the 35 people sentenced to home incarceration were misdemeanants.)

None of the 35 offenders was required to engage in community service or restitution, unless payment of child support is considered restitution. If this interpretation is accepted, three of the 35 were involved in restitution. These three individuals, however, represented 50 percent of the people sentenced to home incarceration because of failure to pay child support. Two of the three paid all of their overdue child support and were current with their child support responsibilities. (Payment of child support is interpreted as an indication of accepting responsibility.)

Five of the 35 offenders either received job training or acquired a job while on home incarceration. One male offender reported that, "Home incarceration gave me the incentive to look for work. That's the best thing that has happened to me in a long time."

Eight of the offenders were required to attend Alcoholics Anonymous; one person was sent to a hospital because of drug problems. These are considered indicators of accepting responsibility.

Overall, it is concluded that the individuals sentenced to home incarceration meet the DOC's objective of having offenders accept their responsibilities to themselves, their families and communities.

An Alternative to Jail

Because of differences in the judges' sentencing philosophies, it cannot be expected that home incarceration would be used similarly. Yet, some evidence was gathered as to whether home incarceration was employed as an alternative to a jail sentence.

Each offender sentenced to home incarceration could have been sent to jail, but was not. This suggests that theoretically home incarceration was used as an alternative to jail. But this does not mean the offender *would* have been sent to jail if home incarceration had not been available as an alternative. The judges, therefore, were asked if they would have sentenced the offender(s) to jail. One judge indicated that it would depend on whether the jail had any space; another judge said "half of the time yes, and half of the time no." The other judge said yes, "except for the offenders who had jobs." It is tentatively concluded that home incarceration was, for the most part, employed as an alternative to jail time.

Net Widening

In Kenton County, home incarceration was not used as a tool for incarcerating more people. With only 35 people sentenced to home incarceration over a year, it would be difficult to conclude that incarceration generally increased. However, if the offenders did not have prior records and were sentenced to home incarceration it *might* be concluded that home incarceration was used to spread "the criminal justice net."

An examination of the records of the people sentenced to home incarceration indicated that 80 percent of the people sentenced had prior jail time. With 20 percent of the people sentenced having never been in jail, it might be possible to conclude that the "criminal justice net" had been extended to include these individuals.

Further examination of the offenders' records produced evidence that this did not occur. Almost 96 percent of the people in home incarceration had prior convictions in Kentucky. Only one person, a male, had no prior convictions. It is therefore concluded that home incarceration with electronic monitoring was not employed to "spread the criminal justice net."

Recidivism

What is the recidivism rate for the offenders sentenced to home incarceration? At this writing not enough time has passed to adequately determine if home incarceration is more or less effective than jail incarceration. However, a control group was formulated of 1984 offenders in Kenton County with similar prior records, age and sex breakdowns. The control group had a 20 percent recidivism rate. Two of the offenders sentenced to home incarceration had been convicted of new offenses, yielding a recidivism rate of 5.7 percent.

Table 3

Prior Jail Time by Sex for Total N

	Male	Female	Total
Yes	27 (77.1)	1 (2.8)	28 (80%)
No	5 (14.2)	2 (5.7)	7 (20%)
Total			35 (100%)

Table 4

Home Incarceration with Electronic Monitoring
Average Days Sentenced by Offense and Sex

	Male	Female
Criminal Mischief	33	
DUI	49	43
Escape/Work Release	180	
Non-Support	39	
Operating on Susp. Lic.	33	
Contrib. Delinq.	28	
Poss. LSD		35
Attempted Burg.	28	
P.I.	30	

This may mean that home incarceration is more effective than jail, but extreme caution is required here because of the small number of cases. The effectiveness of home incarceration with electronic monitoring in reducing recidivism cannot be determined at this time.

The length of an offender's sentence may be related to the effectiveness of the sentence, as well as any special conditions required, such as community service, restitution, treatment or employment. A comparison between the days sentenced to home incarceration and the days an individual would have spent either in jail or on probation without home incarceration suggested that the judges expected the home incarceration sentence to be approximately one-third as long as the alternative sentence. For example, a person sentenced to five months in jail on a revoked driving license was sentenced to 56 days on home incarceration. An offender sentenced to jail for 90 days for driving with a suspended license, received 28 days of home incarceration with no fee.

Reliability of Equipment

The history of the electronic monitoring equipment used in Kenton County is itself an important topic that cannot be fully discussed here. Some of the equipment is outdated because of recent technological developments spurred on by competition in the marketplace, and the desire on the part of consumers to have fail-safe monitoring devices. Never-

theless, it can be concluded that the equipment in Kenton County worked well enough for the type of offenders sentenced to home incarceration.

Several problems were encountered with the equipment. First, about
half of the equipment sent to Kenton County within the first two months
of the project had to be returned to the manufacturer because it malfunc-
tioned or just did not work. This caused interruptions in work schedules,
additional transportation costs and anxiety as to whether the project would
fail because of technological obstacles.

Second, the early computer printouts on offenders were often so garbl-
ed that it became necessary in some instances to call offenders at home
to see if they were absent or present. However, these problems all but
disappeared when the original devices were replaced with much better
equipment from Corrections Services, Inc., Palm Beach, Florida.

The staff responsible for interpreting the computer printouts has become
more knowledgeable because of training and experience. They are now
able to distinguish between a real violation and an apparent violation caused by a "sleeping pattern" or "dead spot" in the offender's home. (For
instance, if an offender is sleeping with one leg on top of the other, the
transmission of a clear signal may be impeded.)

The acid test for the equipment is its detection of actual violations. The
equipment generally did so. Two individuals were returned to jail because
the equipment "caught" them. However, they were not returned only
because the equipment caught them. They were "violated" because of
corroborative evidence.

DISCUSSION

This project was methodologically flawed. In addition to the small sample, the generalizability of the findings was severely limited because the
judges did not sentence people randomly; they were selected on the basis
of each judge's sentencing philosophy. Nor were the sentences for the
control group assigned randomly, thus rendering any definitive comparisons impossible. Other limitations are easily identified, including the
limited time span and the exploratory nature of the project, the use of
only one type of monitoring equipment and only one presentence
investigator.

Nevertheless, the project generated valuable results. It offered an opportunity for testing many ideas about the potential for home incarceration with electronic monitoring, and it contributed immeasurably to
rewriting the 1984 enabling legislation in Kentucky. The remainder of the
paper offers a discussion of the net widening issue, home incarceration

as an appropriate sentence for certain types of chronic misdemeanants and the positive value of Kentucky's 1986 enabling legislation.

Net Widening. While we and others have expressed concern that home incarceration's potential for turning every home into a prison and every bedroom into a cell portends a radical change in the nature of social controls, until now little evidence has been available on this issue. Our limited research suggests this has not occurred. The criminal justice net in Kenton County, Kentucky was not widened, both because of the restrained sentencing policies of the judges, and because those people sentenced to home incarceration had prior convictions. However, we recognize that just because the offenders had prior convictions and sentences does not mean they would have been jailed in the absence of home incarceration and electronic monitoring.

Neither do we know if the judges would have used home incarceration with first-time offenders who could possibly have gone to jail, because these offenders seldom appear before judges for sentencing. These cases are often handled with some form of diversion, including restitution, community service, no contest pleas, "contracts" stating that the charge will be used against the offender should he commit another similar offense, mediation, alternative placements in treatment centers and conditional discharge. In fact, it now appears that the small sample may in part be an artifact of the various opportunities available for avoiding incarceration sentences.

We are somewhat encouraged by this development because it allays some of our fears that home incarceration with electronic monitoring would become a Trojan horse for an increasingly "carceral society" (Foucault, 1977; Ball and Lilly, 1987). Our worst fears have yet to become reality, thus extending our hope that a totally disciplined society will be avoided.

Ironically, however, we find ourselves in the position of not only fearing the net widening effect, but advocating it in some instances. For example, some states allow first-time and persistent drunk drivers to plead to their charge, thus allowing them to return to the community essentially unpunished. This fails to address the public's demand for something more effective; neither does it offer sufficient retribution or protect the community (Ball and Lilly, 1986 a, b, 1987). "Slammer laws" with mandated jail time are equally counterproductive (Ball and Lilly, 1986a). Home incarceration with electronic monitoring addresses both situations. It restricts an offender who might otherwise be unrestricted, yet its restrictions may not be counterproductive. Though we are fearful of the privacy implications of allowing the state to monitor behavior with a machine located some distance from the offender (see Ball and Lilly, 1987), this may be an asset with some types of chronic misdemeanants. Thus, both in symbolic and practical terms chronic misdemeanants represent unique problems.

Chronic Misdemeanants. Chronic misdemeanants represent dual failures. They have not been reintegrated into society, nor has society successfully repudiated their behavior. Home incarceration offers a compromise enabling offenders such as chronic child support defaulters to meet their financial obligations. Jail incarceration had proven ineffective with these offenders, and the state's financial burden was increased by incarcerating the offender. Therefore, the use of home incarceration with other types of chronic misdemeanants should be explored.

Current Law. The 1986 legislation (Kentucky Revised Statute) was markedly different from the 1984 bill, and was broadly supported; it passed with practically no opposition. With only seven sections, it is brief yet revolutionary because it represents (as far as we know) the first enabling legislation in the United States for electronically monitoring offenders. Its provisions merit examination.

Section one addresses the definition of "home," the type monitoring equipment that will be approved and the types of offenders eligible for home incarceration.

The home is defined to include hospitals, hospices, nursing centers, halfway houses, group homes and residential treatment centers. Monitoring equipment may only transmit information as to the prisoner's presence or non-presence in the home. The devices are to be minimally intrusive and incapable of transmitting visual images, oral or wire communications or any auditory sound. Nor will any monitoring device be approved if it is capable of transmitting information as to the prisoner's activities while in the home. With the exception of non-violent felons, only misdemeanants are eligible.

Section two provides that a misdemeanant may petition the court for all or a portion of a sentence, and it limits sentences to not more than six months. It also places home incarceration under the supervision of the county jailer.

Section three establishes the conditions of home incarceration; i.e., when an offender can be absent from the home. It also stipulates that if offenders violate these conditions they can be prosecuted as escapees.

Section four states that violent felons are ineligible.

Section five provides that offenders must be responsible for their own food, housing, clothing and medical care, but they maintain eligibility for government benefits to the same extent as people on probation, parole or conditional discharge.

Section six stipulates that at least once every 30 days the supervising authority shall provide local and county law enforcement agencies with a list of offenders under home incarceration. The information should include each prisoner's place of home incarceration, the crime for which he was convicted, the date for the completion of the home incarceration sentence and the name, address and phone number of the prisoner's supervisor.

Section seven states that the court will establish the conditions of probation and conditional discharge, which could include payment of restitution to the victim. If restitution payments to the victim are required, they will take priority over payments of restitution to any government agency.

The law addresses many of our concerns by specifying conditions of home incarceration, defining the rights of offenders (so they may petition the court), and, most importantly, severely restricting the types of information that may be electronically monitored. The law also provides protection to judges who might have wanted to initiate home incarceration with electronic monitoring but feared public charges of net widening and "big brotherism." The Kentucky law indicates a desire to avoid both problems.

CONCLUSIONS

The Kenton County project on home incarceration with electronic monitoring was a modest success. While the costs of starting the program have not been recovered, it is projected that it is only a matter of time before this occurs.

We conclude that home incarceration is a much more economical form of incarceration than jail. It did not create a financial burden for the citizens of Kenton County, especially in view of the fact that 63 percent of the offenders sentenced maintained jobs which generated taxes, food and shelter. This was accomplished while at the same time protecting the citizenry.

Home incarceration also provided 1,702 days of incarceration outside of the jail, which aided the county judge executive and jailer in their efforts to manage a jail overcrowding problem. While the jail did not experience a depopulation because of home incarceration, it did provide a means by which additional days of incarceration were accomplished. (The jailer would have preferred to have seen home incarceration used more extensively by the district judges.)

The district judges sentenced offenders to home incarceration less than was originally expected. Differences in sentencing philosophies explain the judges' rather conservative use of home incarceration. Nevertheless, the judges and the jailer think that home incarceration is a worthwhile sentencing alternative that should be kept in the criminal justice system.

With 63 percent of the offenders sentenced to home incarceration managing to keep their jobs, and 50 percent of those sentenced because of non-support problems resolving this problem, most of the offenders were assisted in accepting their responsibilities. Others in the pilot program were assisted in accepting their responsibilities by finding employment, attending Alcoholics Anonymous and receiving treatment for drug dependence.

The data also support the conclusions that home incarceration was employed as an alternative to jail time and it was not employed as means of "spreading the criminal justice net." However, it is not possible at this time to determine if home incarceration is more, less or equal to jail in effectiveness. Effectiveness may be associated with the length of home incarceration sentence. Additional research on this point is needed.

Our final conclusion is that the equipment for monitoring offenders worked better near the end of the project than at the beginning. This is explained by the fact the equipment was improved during the course of the project, and the staff became increasingly proficient with the equipment.

REFERENCES

Ball, Richard A. and J. Robert Lilly (1983a). "Home Incarceration: An Alternative to Total Incarceration." Presented to the IV International Meeting of the Society of Criminology, Vienna, Austria.

———(1983b). "The Potential Use of Home Incarceration." Presented at the Annual Meeting of the American Society of Criminology, Denver, CO.

———(1984a). "A Theoretical Examination of Home Incarceration." Presented at the Annual Meeting of the American Society of Criminology, Cincinnati, OH.

———(1984b). "Giving Birth to Electronic Shackles in Kentucky: A Case Study in Creating Law." Presented at the Annual Meeting of the American Society of Criminology, Cincinnati, OH.

———(1985). "Home Incarceration: An International Alternative to Institutional Incarceration." *International Journal of Comparative and Applied Criminal Justice* 9(2):2-19.

———(1986a). "The Potential Use of Home Incarceration for Drunken Drivers." *Crime & Delinquency* 32(2):20-35.

———(1986b). "A Theoretical Examination of Home Incarceration."

Federal Probation L(March):17-24.

———(1987). "The Phenomenology of Privacy and the Power of the State: Home Incarceration with Electronic Monitoring." In *Critical Issues in Criminology and Criminal Justice,* edited by Joseph E. Scott and T. Hirsch. Beverly Hills, CA: Sage.

Calhoun, Jim, (1984). "Kentucky Senate Given Home Incarceration Bill." *Kentucky Enquirer* (January 7),

———(1985a). "Some Legislators Criticize Kenton Jail Program." *Cincinnati Enquirer* (April 11).

———(1985b). "Homing Device: Inmates Wired for 'Home Incarceration.' " *Kentucky Enquirer* (April 20).

Foucault, M. (1977). *Discipline and Punish.* (Translated by A. Sheridan.) New York: Random House.

Kentucky Post (1984). "Let'm Fry a Small Dose." (February 15).

———(1985). "Technology Worth Trying." (January 3).

Kentucky Revised Statute (1986). Section 532:200-250.

Lilly, J. Robert (1985). "A Proposal for Evaluating Home Incarceration in Kenton County, Kentucky." Submitted to the Kentucky Department of Corrections.

Neikirk, Mark (1984). "Electronic Wardens Could Reduce Jail Overcrowding." *Kentucky Post* (December 27).

Straub, Bill (1984). "Home Incarceration Bill Stalled." *Kentucky Post* (March 10).

———(1985). "Lawmakers Question Use of Home Jails." *Kentucky Post* (April 11).

———(1986) "Bill Expands Proposal for In-Home Jails." *Kentucky Post* (January 28).